'Seán's *Customer Intelligence: From Data to Dialogue* book is a concise look at what really matters when a business is serious about driving business value from its most important asset – customer information.'

John McKean, author of *Information Masters* and *Customers are People*, www.informationmasters.com.

'This is an engagingly readable, provocative, and insightful strengthening of understanding of the encouraging relational shift in marketing. It challenges and clarifies misunderstandings of technology's role in buyer-seller interaction. A valuable extension for Relationship Marketing students and anyone intrigued by the apparent power of ICT in business.'

Dr Richard J. Varey, Professor of Marketing, The Waikato Management School, New Zealand.

'*Customer Intelligence* by Seán Kelly is that rare example of a business book that challenges the reader to engage in the debate about the future of marketing in the 21st century. He takes the reader on a fascinating journey from the current impasse between the "build it low cost and they will come" corporate marketers who cling stubbornly to the mass advertising mantra of the past and the pioneering purveyors of customer information strategy who are "betting the business" on the strategy of customer knowledge is power. Global consumers increasingly seek individuality, speed, are more likely to leave you and less likely to listen. Sean has based his analysis on a deep and thoughtful consideration of the challenges facing suppliers in a "buyer-centric" world.

'He identifies how the technical ability of suppliers to reach out to customers is outpacing their marketing insight to do so intelligently. With consumers now migrating from passive consumption to participatory consumption this book challenges the reader to identify the mix of service and flexibility that will characterise the new practice of marketing. I strongly recommend this insightful and readable book to anyone involved in the understanding of customer interactions. To quote the Nobel Prize-winning economist Herbert Simon: "A wealth of information creates a poverty of attention."'

Peter G. Wray, Chairman, 'loyalty matters' and CM4P.

'Every so often, probably not more than once or twice in a decade, a book comes along that succeeds in crystallising a radical change in marketing thinking – what the jargon calls a paradigm shift. In doing so it both defines a moment which will be looked back on later as a seminal point, and sets an agenda for debate and action for years to come.

In the eighties think of Rapp and Collins' *MaxiMarketing*, in the nineties of Peppers and Rogers' *One to One Future*. Halfway through the first decade of the new millennium the book is Sean Kelly's *Customer Intelligence*.

Kelly's elegant, jargon-free style and compelling arguments make the work read like a whodunnit, or in this case a who-didn't-do-it, that both enlightens the thorny questions around why two decades of IT investment have failed to deliver the promised nirvana of close and profitable customer relationships, and offers invaluable pointers on how organisations can finally break through to achieve a new era of customer intelligence.'

Gary Palmer, Fellow, Institute of Direct Marketing, founder of Information Alchemy.

Customer Intelligence

Customer Intelligence

From Data to Dialogue

Seán Kelly

John Wiley & Sons, Ltd

Other Wiley Editorial Offices

John Wiley & Sons Inc., 111 River Street, Hoboken, NJ 07030, USA

Jossey-Bass, 989 Market Street, San Francisco, CA 94103-1741, USA

Wiley-VCH Verlag GmbH, Boschstr. 12, D-69469 Weinheim, Germany

John Wiley & Sons Australia Ltd, 42 McDougall Street, Milton, Queensland 4064, Australia

John Wiley & Sons (Asia) Pte Ltd, 2 Clementi Loop #02-01, Jin Xing Distripark, Singapore
129809

John Wiley & Sons Canada Ltd, 22 Worcester Road, Etobicoke, Ontario, Canada M9W 1L1

Wiley also publishes its books in a variety of electronic formats. Some content that appears in
print may not be available in electronic books

Library of Congress Cataloging in Publication Data

Kelly, Seán, 1960–
    Customer intelligence : from data to dialogue / Seán Kelly.
      p. cm.
    ISBN 0-470-01858-5
    1. Consumers' preferences.   2. Consumers—Research—Data
    processing. I. Title.
    HF5415.32.K45 2006
    658.8'34—dc22   2005019922

British Library Cataloguing in Publication Data

A catalogue record for this book is available from the British Library

ISBN-13 978-0-470-01858-3 (HB)
ISBN-10 0-470-01858-5 (HB)

Typeset in 10/16pt Kuenstler by Integra Software Services Pvt. Ltd, Pondicherry, India
Printed and bound in Great Britain by TJ International, Padstow, Cornwall
This book is printed on acid-free paper responsibly manufactured from sustainable forestry in
which at least two trees are planted for each one used for paper production.

To Meadhbh

Contents

Foreword

When I reviewed this book, it was one of those rare occasions in a domain that I love when I discovered something that had all the ingredients of success written all over it. I have written and published 40 books and have spent many happy hours on publications boards, so I can claim to know a little about what makes a successful business book.

Seán provides a sober account of the information revolution without failing to take into account the real 'counter-revolution' by firms that persist with a bland 'take-it-or-leave-it' attitude to consumers. He is aware that many organizations, such as the banks and oil companies, continue to be mega successful despite their command and control 'inside out' models.

Neither is he naïve about the habits of consumers and does not attempt to persuade his readers that every consumer will want a relationship with their toothpaste manufacturer. Much of life will remain banal despite the revolution in customer information, but some aspects will alter radically. It is his ability to distinguish between the two that makes this book essential reading.

There are two good reasons why this book deserves to be widely read. Firstly, Seán writes brilliant English. It is clear, powerful and focused. He expresses his thoughts lucidly and eloquently. Secondly, the topic of information is generally perceived as boring, largely because people in IS/IT are seen as egocentric, narrowly job-focused, grey and obscure. Never before in my lifetime as a so-called marketing 'Guru' have I found the subject of information so compelling, urbane, relevant and exciting. Seán Kelly, whom I did not know when I first encountered this manuscript, is clearly a genius. His style of writing is riveting; his insights are captivating. He is destined to be one of those authors who change the world.

Professor Malcolm McDonald
Cranfield University School of Management

Acknowledgements

The material contained in this book owes its existence to very many sources. It is rooted in and informed by the author's experience of working with large corporations seeking to build business intelligence systems that will alter the balance of power in the marketplace. To these clients I owe the greatest debt, in no small part because they have provided the primary sources of insight.

The practical experience and intellectual stimulation that informs the book is drawn equally from Europe and the United States and I wish, in particular, to salute the brainstorms and conversations that I have enjoyed on the topic of exploiting information with Tony Butler, Murray Quarmby, Chris Rogers, Joe Oates, Earl Hadden, Roger Burlton, Bill Inmon, Jack Sweeney, Bent Svanholmer, Staffan Elinder and Peter Wray. They are all pioneers in the field of customer intelligence. I also wish to take this opportunity to pay a personal tribute to my late friend and collaborator, Chris Boon, who contributed much of the inspiration and encouragement for this book, but who was destined never to read it.

I'd like to show my thanks for the interaction with my many students over the years at the Data Warehouse Network, The Data Warehousing Institute, DCI, the UK Institute of Direct Marketing, Technology Transfer Italia, NCR, IBM, SAS Institute, the CRMIC and Comhrá Ltd. To all those vendor organisations that have plied their wares in the business intelligence market I also have a debt of gratitude, but especially to my former colleagues in the Sybase business intelligence division.

Above all, I wish here to acknowledge the debt this book and I owe to the many hundreds of managers at scores of companies who have consulted me on the topic of customer information. Every insight of value has its roots in the practical experience gained from collaborating with these business leaders. This book is a tribute to their courage and endeavour and I acknowledge, in particular, those who championed the transition away from mass marketing in their organizations in the early and mid 1990s when it was a radical and uncomfortable stance to adopt.

I also need to acknowledge the patience of John Wiley & Sons Ltd, especially to Diane Taylor for originating this project many years ago, as well as to Sarah Booth and Darren Reed for continuing to support the book at Wiley. Also for the perseverance of all of my colleagues at Comhrá Ltd, especially to Diana Pitcher for continuing, for so many years, to keep me organized.

Finally, having acknowledged those who have contributed most, I wish to pay tribute to those who have endured most. To my wife Nicola I tender my thanks and appreciation for the many days lost to the monomania that is writing a book and to our darling daughter Meadhbh, to whom this book is dedicated, for making her delightful arrival early on in the writing enterprise.

Introduction

Customer intelligence describes the knowledge that an organization has concerning the likely future intentions of its customers or prospective customers. And, since customers no longer respond *en masse* to any particular marketing stimulus, the concept of customer intelligence must encompass a detailed empirical knowledge of the separate components that comprise a given market. Having an intelligence capability allows the enterprise to respond to, (or better still to anticipate), the increasingly fragmented behaviour patterns of customers. And the importance that now attaches to customer intelligence simply reflects the undisputed reality that information is now the decisive weapon of competitive struggle in the marketplace.

The notion of information warfare is not new and military specialists have been examining the implications of information warfare for some time. The military definition of information warfare is concerned with the ability to control access to key information as well as the offensive use of viruses to paralyse an enemy's financial markets or communications systems. In a paper presented to the United States National Defence University in 1996[1] the following is unambiguously stated about the future of military hostilities: 'Those who master the techniques of information warfare will find themselves at an advantage over those who have not; indeed, information warfare will, in and of itself, relegate other, more traditional and conventional forms of warfare to the sidelines'. In the sphere of commercial competition this has already happened. The commercial application of information warfare is more concerned with using superior marketing strategies to disrupt the enemy and the ultimate commercial goal is to create information empires that lock in customers and lock out competition.

The customer information wars that are fought daily in the marketplace are concerned with the ownership and control of information about customers. Competitive advantage rests with those firms that have developed the best skills and capabilities to exploit this information. And, while some casualties have already been carried off the battlefield, the information empires that were anticipated a decade ago have yet to fully emerge. It is not just a war between conventional providers of competing goods and services, but it is a struggle where non-traditional competitors are using superior customer intelligence to enter new markets that were not their traditional preserve. For example, much of what we have witnessed in the information revolution has been a process of re-mediation whereby retailers sell insurance or brand their own goods. Conversely, established businesses that traditionally communicated directly with customers, such as insurance underwriters and manufacturers, are scrambling to preserve relationships with consumers that are increasingly owned and controlled by the intermediary sales channels. Other players are seeking to control access to information by creating dominant positions as information 'portals' where the strategy is to control all crucial information and become the exclusive brokers of information to the providers of goods and services. All these parties are jostling to gain ownership of the customer relationship. And, interestingly, there are many firms that continue to thrive in the absence of any intelligence capability and who have remained largely non-belligerent in the information wars.

Almost one trillion dollars have been spent during the past decade in acquiring, managing and exploiting customer information. The avowed goal of this enormous investment in computer hardware, software, services, applications and internal corporate costs has been to acquire superior customer intelligence. The logical consequence of having such intelligence is to exploit it through greater customization of service. But the promised aims of precise targeting, customer retention, risk mitigation, relationship management and optimized lifetime value exchange seem as elusive as ever. Far from being extinguished by the forces of personalization, the widespread practice of undifferentiated mass marketing continues unabated. From the perspective of many corporate managers there is a tangible sense that the information offensive is bogged down or is, at best, grinding forward in imperceptible increments. From the viewpoint of many consumers who have, wittingly or unwittingly, disclosed their personal information, the promise of individualization has proven illusory, trivial or exploitative.

The primary motivation in writing this book is to ask what we have to show for our efforts and to anticipate where further effort will lead us. It is certainly not the case that nothing of value has been achieved in the exploitation of customer information; many undeniably impressive advances have been made in organizational effectiveness. For example, order management, stock flow, sales pipeline management and financial management have all improved dramatically. But the fact also remains that the personalization of the interaction with the individual customer is far from being a pervasive feature of the market. This raises a number of pertinent strategic issues which include, at least, the following questions.

- Have we applied the principles of mass customization correctly?
- Is the technology too immature or expensive to realize the vision?

- Do we sufficiently understand the intermediary stages between mass marketing and mass customization?
- Is there a common shared understanding of terms like mass customization and personalization?
- Is there organizational resistance to the concept of personalization in the boardroom?
- Is personalization, and the specialization it implies, inimical to achieving the economies of scale required for competitive pricing?
- Can customized and homogenized consumer markets coexist indefinitely?
- Is it possible that the progress made thus far in achieving a more individualized dialogue with customers is capable of being discarded or reversed?
- How do we now redeem the sunk investment made in business intelligence systems in order to realize the original vision?
- Are we on the brink of a major breakthrough that will see the accumulating weight of the information economy vanquish the marketing primitives in our midst?
- Or is there a fatal flaw in our application of the concept of a mass differentiated marketplace?

And, in the end, there is the question that all authors must attempt to answer and it is always the same question, 'what is going to happen next and why?' It will be up to you, the reader, to determine if that question has been answered to your satisfaction and time will anyway, as it always does, provide a brutal scrutiny of the diagnosis and predictions made here.

It is almost 25 years since Alvin Toffler coined the term demassification [2] to describe the eclipse of mass production and mass marketing and seven years later Stan Davis outlined in detail how the concept of mass customization [3] would work in practice. Over a decade ago

Don Peppers and Martha Rogers outlined how the technological tidal wave would usher in a future that would be based on One to One relationships.[4] Shortly afterwards Frederick Reichheld published his dramatic findings on the impact of customer loyalty[5] on profitability. Strenuous efforts were made to intensify customer identity through the use of loyalty cards. At about the same time the concept of customer relationship management (CRM) escalated into a burgeoning industry encompassing every facet of customer interaction. All of the assumptions underpinning these concepts relied on the anticipated impact of information technology. To those of us on the technology side of the fence these visionary voices from the business world were a validation of the value of the customer information that we were quickly learning to manage and analyse. From 1990 the market for business intelligence hardware and software exploded and was driven primarily by the pursuit of customer intelligence. This was followed in the mid-1990s by an amelioration of consumer anonymity during the dot com revolution where every customer declared their identity and trillions of 'cookies' have, by now, been deposited on customers' computers to observe and monitor their behaviour. Between 1990 and 2000 the amount of information stored about customers in the average corporation had increased fiftyfold and the business benefits to be gained from exploiting that data seemed abundantly clear.

As the old verities were swept aside it seemed clear that a new map of the commercial universe was being drawn. There was no doubt that the earth was round and many of the early navigators returned laden with treasure. However, as time passed, more and more explorers ventured forth never to be seen again. This was, of course, unremarkable in a world where many novices were ill equipped and driven by naïve optimism or opportunism. But, now that a decent interval has elapsed, it is time to ask why, if the earth is truly spherical, did so many ships disappear over the horizon never to return and why do the flat earthers continue to assert their dogma with equanimity. This book is, at bottom, an attempt to explain why the age of information has substantially failed to live up to its own hype.

Legislators, industry lobby groups, civil liberties groups and customers have also now entered the fray. As the fog of war thickens it is becoming more difficult for observers, and even for participants, to know what is happening. The confusion that is evident everywhere suggests that this is a war that will rage for the next several decades. It is clear that the stakes are high and those who emerge triumphant can establish an unassailable competitive advantage in the market for a long time to come. It is equally clear that we are now reaching an inflection point that marks the end of the beginning of this conflict for information hegemony. The end of this first phase is marked by the transition from merely acquiring data to actually exploiting it and the manner in which this happens is likely to prove decisive to the final outcome.

Despite all that is done and said in the name of information there is, and always has been, a critical failure by the corporate officers in the modern enterprise to take ownership of data as a strategic business resource. In almost all instances, the customer registration process (and the ongoing process of customer information acquisition) is not designed to improve subsequent marketing but remains a minimalist exercise designed merely to support the particular operational transaction that gives rise to it. The failure to effectively exploit information or to decisively transform the business model from one of mass marketing to personalized marketing is due, in some part, to an irrational focus on technology to the exclusion of business users of that technology. This is important, and is explored in the book at some length, but it is not a sufficient explanation; it does not account for the yawning gap that separates the domain of declared strategic vision and actual operational practice.

Many corporate environments (in common with many military establishments) tend to regard intelligence as a background activity running parallel to the main operations of the enterprise. The intelligence is used from time to time to realign an operational superstructure that is not itself fashioned by, or automatically responsive to, the continuous surveillance of the environment. This leads to a situation where information exploitation initiatives are generally specific and elective episodes rather than systematic or obligatory processes. In such circumstances information is a comfort blanket to which the organization clings in times of crisis. It is used to report against performance rather than to determine direction. It is used to prove or disprove a particular course of action rather than to discover and assess the many courses of action that might be considered. It is perceived as a series of snapshots rather than a continuous flow. And it is treated as a defensive asset rather than an offensive capability. Therefore, the historical tendency in information utilization is to seek to ensure that the enterprise is well regulated rather than genuinely adaptive.

Of course, organizations will become encrvated during periods of trauma when good intelligence is crucial. But there is a marked tendency for the intelligence capability to moulder when the threat induced spasm has passed. It is the response to fear, rather than opportunity, that motivates the enterprise. In this respect, I have highlighted, in the final chapter, what I believe to be a gaping hole in the conventional practice of customer information exploitation. That big gap is the failure to cede ownership of the business-to-consumer relationship to the consumer. In other words, all of our endeavours to date are linear; there is no closed loop that provides the elementary basis for continuity and quality assurance. This encourages the ad hoc and selective use of the information and ensures that there is no need to engage with the customer in a systematic (or contractual) exchange of information for benefits. My reasons for promoting this concept are not just ethical; they are intensely practical as well. If this book has a 'big idea', that is it in a nutshell.

Intelligence is always the decisive factor in war. Those who have the ability to apply a ruthless and accurate logical analysis are more likely to make the right decisions. The real dilemma is that business does not present competing alternatives where the logic tree can fork in two alternative directions, but comprises instead a range of options and interdependencies that fans outwards alarmingly. The topic of information exploitation is so vast that, even when confined to customer information, the canvas extends to include management science, a variety of technologies, process engineering, consumer psychology, cognitive processes, organizational theory, risk management, regulatory instruments, customer-focused initiatives in marketing and the theory of information. I confess to being fully competent in only some of these fields of endeavour and have some trepidation in addressing the entire canvas. However, the persistence of the questions posed by these inter-related disciplines compel me to attempt to pull some of the strands together and attempt a synthesis of the subject matter. In doing so my excuse is that I have lived in the uncomfortable nexus of these overlapping subjects for over a decade and feel entitled to, at least, make a concerted effort at defining the problem and offering some putative solutions. I have not attempted to treat all of the separate topics comprehensively; instead the book is concerned with a synthesis of these issues into a straightforward narrative of how we got to be where we are now and where our next steps will lead us.

When we speak of customer information we must recognize that the customer is simply the fulcrum of the business and that everything from production to supply chain, finance, risk management, personnel management and product development all adapt to, and converge on, the business value proposition that is projected to the customer. Oddly enough, customer information exploitation is a topic that has received relatively little attention in a world much more preoccupied with information systems, information access, information networks and information technology than in the customer information product itself. It is also true to say that there is nothing particularly new about this topic. Customer transaction data has yielded valuable nuggets of intelligence long before data was propelled into cyberspace. E-commerce, where the customer is truly disembodied and can *only* be perceived by their behaviour, simply makes explicit the necessity of converting accurate customer data into useful customer profiles. Having made my own contribution to the technology prejudice with previous publications,[6] this book is also a personal effort to redress the balance.

Much of the public fascination with information has got to do with speed. How quickly we can transmit and receive information is treated with reverential awe. Yet the public is only becoming vaguely aware of how value is added to the information that is transmitted and even less aware of what happens to the data about them that is stored. The information highway is clogged with traffic. But the data that is captured at every portal, visitor centre and toll bridge provides the key to future competitive advantage. This information will become a currency in its own right. Hopefully, it will become the means of constructing meaningful interactions with customers. But there is also a chance that it will contain the seeds of tyranny and it may not just be the data, but the customer, that gets exploited.

It is my intention in this book to provide practical assistance to business practitioners and to steer clear of the two extremes of theoretical abstraction on the one hand and the sterile recitation of case study on the other. I have avoided altogether the temptation to present a grand unifying theory of information exploitation. Nowhere within these covers will the reader find a taxonomy or methodology that can be instantly applied to information strategy. There are no diagrams, formulas, graphs or equations. And I have made an earnest effort to avoid the inscrutable jargon that usually excludes business users from discussions of information technology. At the same time I have assumed, on the part of the reader, an elementary knowledge of marketing and information technology principles. I can only hope that this balance has been struck successfully.

The structure of the book comprises two parts. Part I outlines the current state of play as far as customer information is concerned and attempts to isolate that which has been successful in achieving an environment of customer intelligence. It also examines the critical issues and dilemmas now facing decision makers and how these are likely to be resolved. Part II seeks to isolate the critical success factors that will guide our next steps in utilizing customer information and proposes remedies to the deficiencies and obstacles that have been explored earlier. In identifying that the first stage of customer information utilization spanned the 1990s, and we are now embarked on a second stage, I am acutely aware that very many businesses, perhaps even a majority, are still mired in the first stage. It is also true that the eight separate transitions that are explored chapter by chapter are occurring at a different rate and in a different sequence from one business to the next. Readers should be able to judge from each chapter whether their organization has managed the business transition that is described.

It is unfortunately true, and ominous for readers of this book, that the professions of information technology and marketing have both defied any attempt to impose a scientific rigor on the language employed in their respective disciplines. Thus, the indiscriminate use of common technological terms like information, data, knowledge, system, application, solution and infrastructure have devalued any concrete meaning that might be associated with these words. Likewise, in the domain of marketing any attempt to nail down what constitutes a customer, a relationship, a segment, a profile, a channel or a campaign gives rise to lengthy and generally unproductive debate. For the purposes of this book I have not dared to attempt to regulate this confusion but have observed the discipline of defining what I mean by a term when I use it. The 'CRM' acronym I have tried to avoid entirely, not because it is a flawed concept, but because the multiplicity of interpretations attaching to it has devalued the term beyond any hope of redemption.

This is a book addressed primarily to those engaged in marketing strategy and all those who grapple every day with the challenge of understanding their customers. It is also addressed to business strategists in general and to the information technology management tasked with realizing the business vision of their enterprises. Above all it is a book that is rooted in, and informed by, the author's experience of working with large and small corporations seeking to build business intelligence systems that have altered, and will continue to alter, the balance of power in the marketplace. The book also directs its attention to the general reader, the consumers of the world, who have real fears as well as expectations in the emerging world of information-based commerce. It used to be that customers were the spoils of war; a war engaged in by competing suppliers. But the customer has now become an active participant. Now, more than ever, businesses need customers to cooperate with them in the exchange of information. The failure, by many actors in the information wars, to recognize that the customer has become empowered by the Age of Information is the core theme that is revisited throughout the book. As the temper of the times has changed the message from major consulting and vendor organizations has shifted from championing ambitious strategic initiatives to more modest point solutions. While yesterday's advocates of 'paradigm shift' today speak disparagingly about initiatives to 'boil the ocean' the fact remains that tinkering with a system designed for mass marketing is not going to result in anything other than an increase in contention and confusion.

As yet the Information Age is still just encountered rather than understood. The grammar of information remains unformed and unregulated. Precisely how ubiquitous information will change the way we live has not yet been determined. It is a bewildering landscape littered with the detritus of unexplained failure and success. What is clear is that the strategy and technology choices made by management today will largely shape, not just the future capabilities of their enterprises, but the very economic and social fabric of the world we live in. Information is truly a new frontier. All of you who have ventured forth have done so on the firm assumption that there are vast riches to be discovered on this new continent, but precisely how to distinguish between the treasure and the dross remains challenging. It is my hope that this book will illuminate parts of your journey.

Seán Kelly
October 2005

Part I

The Decade of Customer Information Exploitation

1990–2000

1
The Concept of Customer Intelligence

From Product to Customer

The Concept of a Customer

The single most dramatic aspect of the information revolution has been the extent to which the individual consumer has become an information triggering and transmitting device. Every individual human transaction is monitored and recorded. During the course of the average day many individuals will use an ATM card, a credit card, a telephone, a toll bridge, a loyalty card, a security card, a call centre, digital television or the Internet. On each occasion the transaction data is captured, their selections are noted and the profile of each consumer is further enriched. What consumers do, when they do it and how they do it, is recorded meticulously. Why they do it requires some dialogue with the consumer, but this curiosity is satisfied at present by the armies of market research agencies that engage in polls, surveys and focus groups that seek to determine motivation. Biological human data is also fed through attached and implanted medical monitoring devices and transmitted via mobile phones for remote diagnostics. The human being is now constantly transmitting a stream of data through a variety of channels on a scale that would have been difficult to anticipate even a decade ago. And the data stream continues to grow exponentially. It is this fact that is calculated to dramatically alter the business landscape.

Jonas Riddlestrale and Kjell Nordstrom, the authors of the bestselling *Funky Business* wrote the manifesto of the kaleidoscopic, fragmented, global knowledge society and declared that the individual's desire for recognition is the new pervasive force in commerce. The customer is screaming 'recognize me', 'recognize my lifestyle', 'recognize my life-stage', 'recognize my personal values' and 'recognize my financial value'. 'Fragmentation is largely caused by our wish to belong to and associate with a certain group of people – our desire not to be a commodity, standardized and exactly like the others'.[1] The funky universe describes a society that no longer needs to harbour anxieties about food, shelter or security. The consumer in the mass affluent post-industrial world has ascended the lower levels of Maslow's hierarchy and now demands recognition and opportunities for self-actualization. In such an environment the emotions, sensitivities and values of the individual are paramount and the business challenge is to comprehend (and shape) the 'economies of soul'[2] that are the crystallization of these increasingly globalized shared value systems.

It has been observed that, in circumstances where a relatively small percentage of customers contribute a relatively high percentage of profits the success rate of relationship marketing is improved. This conventional view was driven by the assumption that only valuable customers deserved relationships. Because a high-value skew is unlikely to be true of a business selling newspapers or home heating oil there has been a tendency for such firms to disregard the relationship concept. But this misses the point that developing customer intelligence is not solely concerned with acknowledging value but is also concerned with the potential for design and diversification. Even in businesses where there is not a steep skew, there is every reason to seek to understand what other value propositions might be successfully marketed to the different customer segments that are uncovered.

In the 1950s the management thinker and visionary Peter Drucker (1994) wrote 'there is only one valid definition of business purpose: to create a customer'. For any business to thrive it must pursue a strategy that gains more customers, keeps existing customers and increases the frequency and value of transactions. Achieving these four goals is the purpose of any business. The reality is that most large service companies continue to be beguiled by the management theories of the past and worship devoutly the holy trinity of price advantage, distribution control and economies of scale. These are the mantras of the mass marketing era where customers are a renewable resource and where it is assumed that their behaviour is totally predictable and driven exclusively by price, quality and convenience. In this world view, because the customer is assumed to have a conditioned response that is totally predictable, any effort to study customer behaviour is considered to be a fruitless endeavour. Over the course of time mass marketing companies became aware of an irritating tendency by small groups of customers to not conform. These customers were generally dismissed as 'market niches' and were only addressed by large corporations, not out of any particular interest in the niches as such, but because the existence of the unprotected niche communities allowed for the possibility of new entrants to gain a foothold in the core market.

In 1997 the US banking industry recognized the dramatic growth of information-based banking and described this phenomenon as 'relative newcomers relying on superior knowledge of the customer to strip business after business from traditional players'.[3] The study containing this observation went on to list three reasons why customer intelligence was becoming critical to building competitive advantage. The first reason was because traditional profit guideposts (such as customer tenure, income and demographics) were, by now, misleading indicators of profitability. Secondly, there was a tendency towards dispersal of the financial relationship whereby customers who had previously performed all their business through a single bank now tended to have many service providers and relationships. The third reason was the fact that market rationalization had led to dispersion in value among customers (often leaving a small minority of existing customers subsidizing the remainder) with the consequence that the traditional banking institution was vulnerable to raiding by competitors.[4]

Customers are not bound by price-based value propositions or even by contractual obligations but by the systemization of highly flexible service-based relationships in the life of the consumer that anticipate and serve their needs. In this sense the average consumer and typical business are alike in their desire to outsource non-core activities. The core activity of a consumer is living their lives to the full. The time it takes to evaluate their insurance cover, purchase their staple groceries, check their stock prices, select a telephone call plan, determine the cheapest mortgage or keep up-to-date in their profession or leisure interests are all necessary chores that they would prefer someone else to perform for them. The time they waste in repeating information that they have already supplied to service providers is frustrating. Being asked to provide personal information (on the Internet, in questionnaires or by using so-called loyalty cards) where there is no clear value is intolerable. Having one's time wasted receiving unsolicited and irrelevant messages for value propositions that are not intended for them personally has become a source of incandescent rage. The value of time is now recognized, as it never has been before, by the consumer. For businesses to ignore this reality is to court disaster. Yet, astoundingly, the quantity of unsolicited contacts increases apace all the time. Interpreting this paradox requires us to acknowledge just how deeply rooted is the product-centred culture that is being challenged.

The Concept of a Product

Time was when a product was a simple tangible thing that was delivered in a package and cost a specific amount of money. For some while now this has not been true and it grows less true with each passing year. A product now can be an intangible service. For example, a product bundle, a customized pricing plan, an addition to a product such as a warranty or credit scheme, a version of a product or service, a discount, or a promotion are all classified as products. The three Ss of the mass production culture – standardization, simplification and specialization – continue to define the core product. But the ancillary aspects of products and the packaging of value propositions around products are increasingly important for businesses to understand. As competition drives the price of core products down close to costs, and as technology has the effect of commoditizing products, the profitability of a business is, increasingly, more dependent on these aspects of a product than on the core product itself. More and more, there is a tendency to sell the basic product free or 'at cost' with all profits arising from the personalization factors. For example, it is a widespread practice for mobile phone companies to give away free cellular phones, while the market for personalized ringing tones and icons is estimated to be one billion dollars in Europe alone.

Checking into a hotel and liberally consuming the services on offer is a good guide to the range of things that we call products. In financial terms and in terms of the automation systems that capture data about transactions, a product is normally defined in terms of an entity that has a price or tariff associated with it. Products may be categorized in a hierarchy with category names that describe groups of products which reflect a summarized total revenue stream (e.g. leisure services, business services, booking services). In a world where we are charged each time we use a service there is an explosive increase in the volume of data that is captured about consumers. Not only are the physical outlets for shopping likely to diminish in importance but the ownership of physical products is also likely to diminish. It is irrational in an information environment for people to want to 'own' things in the way that was common in the past; instead people will be satisfied with consuming things. Products like music, books, videos, games, road usage, financial services, telephony and software are all evolving to a subscription-based business model rather than a product sales model. This transaction 'atomicity' will result in each separate transaction being regarded as a product sale. The ISP that charges by time used rather than on a flat rate for a calendar period has a greater incentive to discover what sites its subscriber is visiting, since income in a pay-per-use model is infinitely capable of being stimulated. An ISP that charges a flat monthly rate regardless of usage is, by contrast, not encouraged to examine customer behaviour since it in no way increases revenue directly.

Knowing what business to be in (i.e. what products to sell) is a key benefit of being information-aware. But equally important is to know what part of the market is most responsive to the product. Even well managed financial services companies suffer from the twin threats to competitive advantage which are (a) a tendency to pass on profitable business because of the absence of risk-related information and (b) a tendency to be blindsided to movements in the market due to the absence of customer-related information. Tackling these issues has proved complex for most retail financial institutions because the solution lies in the integration of data that is often hopelessly fragmented across the enterprise. The pan-corporate blending of data has raised thorny organizational questions such as 'who really owns the customer relationship?' or even the more basic question 'what is a customer?'. In a world structured around products and accounts these questions begin to challenge many cherished assumptions in the traditional organization. In the emerging e-business financial services enterprise all processes revolve around customers, adding further urgency to the task of reengineering the traditional businesses. The conventional business assumption, that products are fixed and channels are physical, is being shattered. As the crude tools of mass marketing are abandoned they are replaced by the information-oriented strategies that will fuel competitive advantage in the next decade. As the information content of products increases, then our ability to version and customize products will become just as easy as it is to version and customize software.[5]

Don Peppers and Martha Rogers in their influential book *Enterprise One to One* make a useful distinction between independent purchase events and conditional purchase events. This distinction locates the traditional marketing organization inhabiting a perspective that perceives all customer purchases as independent events unconnected to other purchase events. In this scenario the customer is a renewable resource – since every purchase event is independent then the task of the organization is simply to have a value proposition that appeals to certain customers and to find the customers who are responsive to that value proposition. Translated into operational processes what this means is having a product-led enterprise culture and basing competitive positioning primarily on price. As Peppers and Rogers observed, 'this results in products being priced to attract the last, most marginal, least interested customer'. The alternative approach is to base business strategy on the assumption that most purchases are conditional events. What this means is that the customer retains a memory of the enterprise from one purchase to the next and that the relationship can be enhanced and reinforced through differentiated marketing and pricing. Instead of selling a product at the lowest possible price, the customer-centred organization will tend to offer a range of tailored products to customer segments at a price that reflects the value of that customer to the enterprise.

The Concept of Intelligence

Intelligence is defined as being 'endowed with the faculty of reason' and it is this sense of what is rational and derived from knowledge, as opposed to what is random, superstitious or derived from chance, that differentiates the intelligent from the less intelligent. So, by this yardstick, is the commercial ecosystem[6] in the early 21st century intelligent? To answer this question requires us to determine if the relationship between consumer and supplier in the marketplace is a fully, or largely, rational and predictable relationship. Rationality is not a substitute for excellence and, therefore, we are not concerned here with the 'goodness' of the product or service but rather with its 'sanity'. The simple test of sanity is whether the business communications to its actual and prospective customers are consistent with the actions of the business and with the requirements of the customer. This is the starting point in making our assessment.

The critical issue to be aware of when assessing levels of intelligence is the one of perspective. The intelligence, or lack of it, should be determined solely by the customer's experience. Traditionally, it was the supplier's view of its own capabilities, or a comparative analysis of the capabilities of many competing suppliers, that was used to determine the degree of intelligence of an enterprise. Therefore, the conventional product-centred measures of business performance (such as basket analysis, yield analysis and margin analysis) are giving way to customer-centred measures (such as loyalty analysis, value analysis and lifecycle analysis). The new measures reflect a shift from the trial-and-tempt approach of the market share goal with the retention-and-reward policy of the customer share goal. What we have witnessed during the course of the past decade is a change in the commercial centre of gravity from product to customer. This is proving to be a painful transition for many businesses because many management actions, which are directed at the conventional goals of increasing market share and reducing costs, are often irrational when viewed from the perspective of consumers seeking long term relationships.

Despite massive investments during the past decade in a wide variety of information systems, there is no compelling evidence of commensurate improvement in consumer satisfaction. The experience of most consumers is one that prompts consternation as they grapple with more and more junk mail, unsolicited calls, invasions of privacy and failure to maintain an accurate profile or any profile. Customers are targeted more frequently certainly; but often they are targeted with less accuracy than ever before. For many consumers, the business of doing business has not become demonstrably more intelligent. This is largely explained by the fact that many businesses invested heavily in customer contact systems without having also invested in the intelligence systems that could guide the contacts.

Of course, a significant number of prominent businesses have earned the right to be classified as 'intelligent' and these businesses are making significant inroads in their markets. But they are still a minority and there is no sign that they are trailblazing a single new paradigm that will automatically be followed by all businesses. This is particularly perplexing since many business leaders have declared themselves to be committed to the deepening of customer relationships. Indeed, having invested heavily in data analysis, process reengineering, e-commerce, relationship marketing, call centres, contact management systems and a plethora of other corporate initiatives, many of today's business leaders are themselves perplexed at the failure to achieve significant culture and process change.

The call centre phenomenon has, in the manner of its implementation, been largely self-defeating, and is a good example of management confusion on the subject. There were two possible benefits of a centralized call centre from the point of view of the business and only one possible benefit from the consumer perspective. The two benefits from the perspective of the business were that the call centre would reduce costs and increase revenues. Costs would be reduced by centralizing a fragmented function that was scattered across branches and departments in a single location. Revenues would be increased by cross-selling and up-selling to inbound callers as well as by using the call centre operators for out-bound 'telemarketing' when they were not dealing with inbound traffic. Well, with respect to the cost reduction driver it is clear that the business website is an even cheaper way of disseminating routine information. And the revenue benefit never materialized because the customer profile information was rarely delivered and consumer hostility to 'blind' telemarketing is universal. The consumer benefit was the much heralded 'single-point-of-contact' benefit that would prevent consumers being passed from one department to another. It is quite clear that this was rarely achieved and that the consumer experience of call centres is almost universally negative. The customer profile available to the call centre operator is seldom integrated, the empowerment of operators is close to zero, the extent of training of call centre personnel is superficial and it is frequently the case that the customer is passed on to another function within the call centre. As a source of static data providing responses to simple pricing, order status, quotation or product queries the call centre works quite well. But this is information that is more easily obtained from a well-designed website.

The only compelling case that can be made for human interaction between customer and business is when the issue raised by the customer is complex and this is precisely what the existing call centre model cannot deal with. It is highly unlikely that the call centre as we have come to know it will survive long and will be progressively replaced by the Internet as the numbers of web-phobic older customers drops below critical mass. It is likely that small centres of competence will replace the vast call centre operations to deal with those queries that cannot be satisfied by an intelligent website. Perhaps it is not so surprising that the call centre has not met expectations since it was originally introduced to address blatant failures in the existing fragmented business processes underpinning marketing, sales and customer service. This fragmentation is nowhere more evident than when visiting a marketing technology exhibition. The visitor will be greeted by vendors with solutions for data management, data integration, data cleansing, geodemographic data, lifestyle data, contact management, click stream analysis, segmentation, data mining, campaign management, campaign execution, web design, e-commerce, wireless messaging, behaviour analytics, regulatory compliance, mapping software, retention applications, document management, list brokering, workflow management, computer telephony and call centres. This fragmented, overlapping and bewildering array of options is in marked contrast to the degree of integration that has been achieved in the manufacturing, logistics and financial functions of the enterprise. One of the enduring legacies of the model of mass marketing has been the separation of the marketing and sales functions. This was logical enough in a universe where marketing had no direct communication with individual customers; became inefficient with the advent of direct marketing and now makes little sense at all.

Change is a constant condition of organizations in an open market. As soon as the business hones one value proposition the risk is that the rules change and the proposition becomes obsolete or is directed at the wrong audience. External change constantly threatens mind-numbing ferment as firms constantly reinvent themselves. But the human and corporate psyches have only got a limited capacity for shock. What corporations require is not the ability to be able to respond to change but the ability to anticipate it and incrementally adapt to prevailing conditions. Better still is the firm that can precipitate change. To achieve this we need to have information tools that can behave as the corporate radar. This is the nub of intelligence. It is recognition of the fact that change is not a threat; surprise is.

Inverting the Business Model

The conventional business model has always been a command model. Even those firms that aspire to putting the customer first and placing a premium on the customer relationship often persist with a command structure that is oriented to products. Indeed, most e-commerce also continues to reflect this traditional model of the business. It is a model that says 'we have certain well-defined products and services that may be of interest to you. In addition, we have a number of non-negotiable rules and procedures and if you, the customer, consent to jump through these hoops, then we can do business together'. This attitude of mind reflects a traditional and deeply ingrained culture that is firmly centred on the product or service rather than on the customer. It is also a culture that is consciously inflexible since the business is concerned to match customers to its range of products rather than being concerned with finding the products that are required by the customer. The company manages its business risk by policing the rules and regulations that are set within the bureaucratic policy parameters of the business. The business organization is characterized by high levels of centralized authority, regulation and audit of procedure and low levels of skill and delegated authority at the customer interface. This is the dominant and pervasive business model that we encounter today and is a classic inside-out perspective. Those who reside inside the business entity define how the relationship will function and the consumer is invited to take it or leave it.

A range of innovations in business practice now robustly challenge this conventional wisdom. Chief among these innovations is the substitution of the product focus with a customer focus. In the customer-centred enterprise measures such as share of wallet become as important as share of market. Once the customer is placed at the centre of the business model a fundamentally different question gets posed. Instead of asking how many more prospects can we match to our fixed and inflexible value proposition, the question now becomes one where we ask how many more value propositions can be matched to each customer or customer segment. In effect, the business perspective shifts to being an outside-in perspective.

Making such a transition from an inside out to an outside in business process framework[7] has significant consequences for the business. These consequences include the need to diversify the range of products that the business has to offer, a radical reengineering of the organizational structure to reflect the need to serve groups of customers rather than to promote categories of product and a fundamental reordering of the performance metrics of the business.

But the single most important of these consequences is the need to improve the intelligence that is garnered concerning the consumers that are the target of the business. Having reached a comprehensive understanding of the factors that influence customer loyalty does not necessarily provide a sound basis for business strategy. The concern about 'loyalty' is no more than recognition that a relationship exists between consumer and business and that the sales event 'merely consummates the courtship'.[8] It is not until the measures of loyalty have been combined with measures of profitability, behaviour and lifecycle that the complete customer profile emerges.

The experience of this author in working with companies who are embarked on the journey of information discovery suggests that even the most visionary of business leaders respond with white knuckled shock to discoveries that were waiting to happen. Take a US office equipment chain that discovered that 20% of their customers considered the cost of acquiring a printer cartridge with a ticket price of $20 to be in excess of $60. What these customers were calculating was the cost of their time and the inconvenience of having to go to a store during working hours. Or the European energy distribution company that discovered that a mere 0.5% variation in energy prices would result in an attrition level of 25%. Or the hotel chain that discovered that the main complaint from business travellers was that they wanted to have the use of office services outside of office hours (when they were actually in the hotel).

The shock of discovery can result in a number of scenarios. Business leaders can decide that this is a golden opportunity to redesign the business to accommodate the exigencies of customers and, as no two customers are the same; this inevitably leads to differentiation in service, process, price and product. But the shock of discovery does not always result in an engagement strategy that embarks the enterprise on the road to customization. In very many instances discovery is followed by denial. It has been the unremitting experience of this author that many business leaders faced with new incontrovertible facts about their customers or their market react with unease and scepticism rather than excitement. To executives schooled in the old ways, who have developed their reputations as cost-cutters, the challenge of mass customization looms like a Byzantine complexity that is too terrifying to contemplate. The appalling vista that dawns on many business executives is that a business that surrendered to such customer demands would be run by the IT department! What business leaders need to decide is whether they really want to struggle for control with a customer in a relationship. Customers have control because they can leave.

Customization of marketing messages and relationships mark a significant transition away from mass marketing. Achieving the level of customer intimacy required to engage in one-to-one communications requires substantial investment in the business intelligence systems that are used to discover the events, trends and patterns in the data that allow the supplier to fully comprehend (and even to anticipate) the needs of customers. Any genuine attempt to engage in customer retention, up-selling, cross-selling or product bundling strategies requires sophisticated business intelligence software and a substantial overhaul of marketing processes within the enterprise. And, having embarked on this transition, there has to be a recognition that one likely outcome is widespread diversification of the business.

It should be observed that many organizations are opting to evade the transition to customer-centred processes by defining an ever larger range of customer services while firmly retaining the command structure. A good example of this would be the many hotel chains that now offer an extraordinarily comprehensive range of guest services and where each service is described and defined in detail. One assumes that the goal of such a policy is the definition of every conceivable request that a customer might make and to define a programmed response to each case. But the fact that this results in a very comprehensive list of services does not disguise the truth that it nonetheless remains an inflexible menu, albeit a very comprehensive one. A guest who requests a shoe-shining service where this is not one of the many services on offer will be met with blank incomprehension and a yawning gap will continue to exist between disguised product-centred systems and genuinely customer-centred ones.

At one extreme are market pirates; businesses that exist to exploit a temporary need in the marketplace where no intention exists to offer any value proposition or to build enduring relationships. While this business model is highly exploitative (and often highly profitable) the pirate enterprise is normally short lived. The working assumption of the pirate enterprise is that, at some stage, it will cease to exist. At the other extreme are organizations that exist solely to have and maintain a relationship with its customers. Voluntary associations, charities, not-for-profit organizations and religious organizations can all be located in this category. The underlying assumption here is that, while the organization will have to evolve; it has no intention of ceasing to exist. The global transition from product to customer may be seen in the context of moving from a business instinct focused on opportunity to a business instinct informed more by service. In a marketplace where consumer sophistication is steadily growing customers are more readily equipped to make this distinction. However, given the complexities of the market and the turbulence that attends to every major business change, it is highly probable that, during the course of this transition, a temporary opportunity will be created for a counter movement.

The Counter Revolution

After a decade of substantial and growing investment in improved customer intelligence the turn of the millennium marked a downturn in commitment to customer management. Frustration at the complexity and disappointment at the results of tentative customer management initiatives explains some of the counter trend. The fact that every study of customer loyalty cited inertia as a more important factor than satisfaction also accounted for increased complacency. It was also the case that businesses recognized that external shocks that redefined the marketplace presented a greater threat to survival than the defection of customers to competitors. And, largely due to the effect of new technology, improvements in supply chain management presented dramatic opportunities in some sectors to gain significant price competitiveness on a scale that trumped any service quality advantages enjoyed by competitors. To the hard-boiled business executives who never had much patience anyway with customer loyalty initiatives the real source of success in business is determined by clout (favourable regulatory treatment or control of channels), glitz (sports sponsorship and celebrity endorsement), value (cutbacks and more cutbacks) and happenstance (population growth and economic expansion). The one thing they are sure of is that coddling customers has got nothing to do with it. The assumption of the counter revolutionaries is that growth is determined by price, brand affinity, product quality and service quality, in that strict order. And because customer intelligence initiatives are perceived to be costly, and therefore a threat to price competitiveness, it is unsurprising that service quality often falls off the list entirely.

The discounters have been able to dominate the great centre of the consumer bell curve only because the incumbent players have ceded this space in the market. Indeed, it remains a curiosity of the consumer markets that established retailers seem to be subject to a mysterious magnetic force that progressively draws them into the congested space at the premium end of the market, while remaining incapable of developing strategies that maintain their appeal to multiple market segments simultaneously. This phenomenon is easily explained by the central obsession that branding occupies in the minds of consumer marketers, but the failure to recognize the trap inherent in monotone branding is not as easy to understand.

The counter revolution has its own ideologues as well. Stephen Brown has written an entertaining manifesto for hucksters that lampoons relationship building as 'tantamount to stalking' and revels in the fact that good old fashioned 'glitz and glamour' marketing is more art than science.[9] Of course, there is nothing mutually exclusive about relationship marketing (to build intelligence) and creative marketing (to build brand awareness). What is interesting is the visceral antagonism displayed by many advocates of creative marketing for the dry mathematical precision of scientific marketing. For Brown, success in marketing campaigns proceeds from 'a deeper understanding of what people want than would ever emerge from the bowels of a data mine'.[10] Heroes of the creative marketing faction include the creator of the scarce and collectable Beanie Babies, the makers of the tantalizingly ambiguous *Blair Witch Project* movie or Pizza Hut who garnered publicity by paying for their logo to be emblazoned on a Russian space rocket. These are indeed fine examples of good old-fashioned creative marketing and follows on the venerable tradition of jolting or manipulating the market that is as long as history itself. But much creative marketing is less benign than these examples and is frequently devoted to obfuscating the value proposition. The real professionals of caveat emptor marketing are to be found in the ranks of those who separate high net worth individuals from their wealth by extending 'privileged' access to expensive limited-edition products and 'exclusive' access to risky financial investments. Without doubt, ingenuity can stretch a meagre marketing budget and a carefully managed 'exclusivity' will always find, amongst the affluent and adolescent, a frenzied desire to have what ones' peers have not. But such stunts rely for their effect on the recurring gullibility of the few or the sporadic euphoria of the many. Consumers in the broader market have a limited capacity to be shocked, affronted or tantalized. The success of the three-card trickster is that he comes to town once a year on festival day when people have a propensity to be amused. There is a clear understanding that when the tents come down, he moves on. It is not a trick that you can keep repeating.

The sweet spot in the market is a moving target. Knowing where it is (and where it is going to be) is the essence of business strategy in the adaptable firms that are not in the business of persuasion but in the business of matching value propositions to pliable customers in the profitable sweet spots in the market. Hyper-profitable companies have not achieved their status by micro engineering their processes, cultures or products but by being in the right place at the right time. But hyper-profitability is not a long-lived phenomenon and the basic business premise that exploits temporary opportunity does not make for a durable business strategy.

Instead of the technology-enabled shift away from the numbing standardization of the mass marketing culture that was widely anticipated, there is strong evidence that the opposite has occurred. Not for the first time in history has the real world veered sharply away from the path anticipated by experts and commentators. Some of the reasons for this have, no doubt, to do with the flaws and deficiencies in the application of the new technology that were discussed earlier in this chapter. Other drivers of the counter revolution include new technological developments such as the phenomenon of SPAM[11] that is disfiguring e-mail on the Internet. But we are not dealing here with an inadequate or incomplete realization of the vision of customization; we have to soberly acknowledge that an actual trend reversal is taking place.

The 'age of information' promised more specialization, greater variety, greater personalization and substantially improved quality of service. The new generation of marketing executives that arrived on the scene a decade ago promised not simply to satisfy their customers, but to surprise and delight them. New technologies would allow us to discard the primitive 'catch-all' messages of mass marketing and there was excited talk about the marketing possibilities presented by the market segment of one customer. In a universe where individual consumer needs could be identified, personalization would replace homogenization.

In reality, the past decade has witnessed a marked trend by large numbers of highly successful businesses in the polar opposite direction. Everywhere can be seen to be a move away from variety and towards specialization. Variation, it seems, is the enemy of process simplification. While process variation may seem relatively straightforward and highly desirable in principle the perceived costs that are associated with process complexity had not been adequately anticipated by those predicting a mass customized future. Hidden costs in a complex process include staff training, operator specialization (with attendant scheduling complexity, training complexity and increased hazard of demarcation conflict), organizational fragmentation, computer systems complexity as well as embedding costs in procurement and supply chain. The general trend in retailing, in so far as the application of technology is concerned, is towards fragmentation. While some retailers are forging ahead with ambitious loyalty card, e-tailing and one-to-one sales strategies, others, who have been less than impressed by their forays into technology-led initiatives, are growing more cautious and, in some cases, actually abandoning technology initiatives. In the airline industry many carriers have downgraded or even abandoned their loyalty schemes in the face of a savage onslaught (particularly in Europe[12]) from the 'no frills' budget airlines. Even where reward schemes have been retained, many airlines have begun to talk of these frequent flier programs as a 'burden'.

The drive for personalization has no force independent of the technological means that can enable this innovation. The curiosity is that the technological means exist and can be considered to be reasonably mature. Yet, the drive towards personalization is undeniably stalled as evidenced by a growing, rather then a reducing, volume of undifferentiated marketing communications. It is not simply the SPAM that clogs up every e-mail user's inbox or the irritating interruptions to everyday life occasioned by telemarketing campaigns; it is also that the vast majority of mainstream business-to-consumer enterprises in banking, retailing and telecommunications have demonstrably failed to convincingly make the transition from mass marketing to mass customization. The evidence is also apparent in disappointments that companies report in investments that they have made in business intelligence systems as well as the relatively short-lived experiments we have witnessed in customer relationship management.

'It's the price, stupid' appears to be the loud response from the product-centred advocates. But even this obvious driver does not explain the success of all product-centred businesses. Many businesses that are focused on upscale (i.e. not price sensitive) consumers demonstrate the same narrow focus that typifies the budget enterprise. Many exclusive restaurants would greet a request for a hamburger with the same degree of incomprehension as a fast food restaurant would greet an order for liver pâté. Service excellence is not cumulative.

It is simply a different specialized niche. This evidence strongly suggests that the mass market is redefining itself, not in terms of membership by customers of multiple segments at one time or during their lifecycle, but with business strategies that are exclusively focused on individual segments. While these phenomena demonstrate that progress toward a culture of individualization will not necessarily proceed in a unilinear fashion, there is little doubt that the ultimate destination that is enabled by technology is a market segment of one being served by an integrated suite of services. Since the base technology to achieve this is, in fact, already substantially mature, the inevitable question is 'what is impeding progress towards this goal?'

Many apparently plausible explanations can be advanced to explain why the business adoption of individualized marketing lags so far behind the technological capability to deliver it. These include concerns about privacy, the usual problems of organizational inertia in the face of cultural change, as well as the data integration challenge faced by large organizations with many legacy information systems. There is also some evidence that customization capabilities that had been successfully developed have subsequently failed to survive company mergers in circumstances where the partner to the merger did not have a similar capability.

There is also the problem that much of the hype surrounding individualization and relationship marketing has confused the issue in a number of fundamental respects. A key misconception that is frequently touted is that individualization will facilitate a return to the cosy small-town relationship between customer and supplier. It will not. System-driven customer care infrastructures can only enable differentiation options that are programmed into the system. It will never be a substitute for the personalized care of the empowered and highly flexible proprietor owned enterprise. System-driven customer care based on individual preferences and requirements will always be systematic and will never have the cachet of the small town storekeeper or luxury goods provider where the relationship between customer and supplier is based on a longstanding personal relationship between two human beings. To be sure the enormous gap in individual care that currently exists between the luxury market and mass market will diminish dramatically. It may even prove to be the case that the mass customized enterprise serving a mass market will prove to be more pampering of the customer at a tangible and quantifiable level. But the person-to-person contact will always command a premium and will always be able to promote intangible qualitative distinctions. The luxury end of the market may well have to work harder to justify their margins and there will be some corrosion of this sector since many rational consumers will fail to see the value in a highly individualized expensive service when compared to a highly individualized economy service.

Of course, much of the counter revolution is nothing more than a return to the age-old business practice of focusing exclusively on the mass at the centre of the market. The model of the product-centred enterprise is to find customers for a product and not products for customers. Success in this model rests on doggedly refusing to be enticed into serving the differing needs of those occupying the trailing tails of the normal distribution bell curve. Regardless of the potential of technology, keeping it cheap and keeping it simple are perceived to be the prime survival goals. The counter revolutionaries fear that matching smaller and smaller segments with ever larger menus of options does run the risk of resulting in an exponential complexity; and that complexity equals high costs and uncompetitive prices.

What this tells us is that there is considerably less real competition in the marketplace than we might be inclined to believe. For many business executives profit comes from cost-cutting and control of channels which in turn comes from synergies achieved though market share growth which in turn comes from mergers and takeovers. In these circumstances customers are not won over by superior service; they are the spoils of war. Like medieval serfs they have no say in their allegiance. They simply belong to territory won during the course of commercial conflict. They are not agents of their own destiny but are allocated through affairs of state. They are essentially disloyal and are responsive to price. They may revolt if rents are too high but otherwise are not worthy of too much consideration. This is a tough mindset to change and it is a mindset that is shared by more business enterprises than would care to confess to such opinions. 'Customers are a renewable resource' was the astounding observation of a large retail chain manager who made the comment only slightly tongue-in-cheek. The perception is that there are always new markets to be conquered. With enormous latent demand in their home markets most enterprises in North America and Europe are more concerned with the 'new' markets in China and elsewhere. That there will forever be new frontiers is the earnest hope of the product-centred marketers.

Operational necessity is the prime driver of any business organization and the constant operational necessity has always been cost reduction. Any attempt to harvest customer information within a cost-cutting culture is directed at fine tuning a supply chain that perceives the customer as a mildly oscillating handle driving the process. And, within such a mindset, the solitary point of an information economy is to reduce the gap in time and distance between producer and consumer. Indeed, retailers will soon dispense with checkouts entirely when customers are persuaded to use radio frequency identification (RFID) technology that automatically scans purchased goods and enables payment authorization. The Internet has already eliminated vast swathes of supply chain complexity. Simplification removes expensive handoffs and improves demand feedback from the market. The resultant cost savings of these 'efficiency factors', it is asserted, drives competition forward with more momentum than can be unleashed by 'loyalty factors'. The frictionless economy creates vivid transparency as local monopolies; customer ignorance; lock-in devices and general inertia all disappear in the clear light of the global comparable market. Enormous efficiencies are realized as the information economy vaporizes the complex network of dependencies that characterized the 'old' economy.

But as Gary Hamel, the management scientist, has observed, 'the hard truth is that most companies owe a good portion of their profits to friction. Friction inflates prices. Friction reduces competitive rivalry. Friction protects margins. So for many companies, the profit boosting benefits of the Web-driven efficiencies will be overwhelmed in the price-deflating effects of ever less friction'.[13] In other words, a new equilibrium will emerge and, in the end, comparable value propositions will have to be differentiated with reference to the obvious remaining variable – the customer. In a totally transparent market that new equilibrium will be brutal and unforgiving and customer demand in this enlarged market cannot continue to be accurately measured as if it were a suggestible homogenous mass that erased its own memory at the completion of every transaction. Neither can assumptions be made about an enduring inertia on the part of customers. Inertia has less to do with a psychological complacency on the part of consumers than it has to do with carefully constructed exit barriers placed in their way by business. When, for example, number portability was forced on a reluctant telecommunications industry by regulators, customer churn exploded. As the current round of operational efficiencies is being digested and operational processes become ever more fine-tuned, attention is shifting urgently to discover how to eliminate those unexpected oscillations, surges and outages that continue to short circuit the entire system. However, as businesses learn to respond to the many different pulses in the market there will undoubtedly be further reductions in supply-chain friction, but cost efficiencies will not be the primary driver of customization; customer retention will. The new operational imperative will be to create friction through customization features that maintain customer loyalty. We are rapidly approaching the point when all of the surviving competitors achieve comparable levels of information-induced cost efficiencies. And when that point is reached each competing business will turn its gaze to the enormous mass of customer data that has been dammed up behind the walls of an outdated operational necessity.

The fact that the overall level of quality, reliability and range of product choices has steadily improved for most consumers during the past decade should not distract from the fact that the apparent range of options available to consumers has, in very many cases, been diminishing over the same time. Given all the brouhaha about building customer relationships it is sobering to note that it took the threat of terrorism rather than sincere concern for customer service to persuade airlines in the US to take the basic step of linking every piece of baggage on an airline to an actual passenger.[14] Mass customization holds out the promise of large-scale operations coexisting snugly with an intimate and personalized service. The key message of one-to-one marketing is that mammoth scale is not synonymous with customer alienation. Large can be beautiful. However, the potential for large-scale low-cost operators to provide mass customized service offerings is being ignored in the headlong rush to achieve size simply for the sake of cost-effective synergies. But it is also important to note that the actual volumes of customer data that is accumulating in many of the low cost businesses that are oriented to electronic interactions is actually greater than the data being amassed by traditional businesses. Therefore, when these businesses choose to switch their focus to customers, and they surely will, they will be proceeding from a position of considerable strength. For even the discounters are aware that sustained competition that is based exclusively on price is the road to dusty death for most competitors in the market. This natural inclination will, in any event, feed the desire for differentiation attributable to service-oriented factors.

The Myth of Bifurcation

But just as there has been a reaction away from customization so too has there been a reaction away from standardization. The Spartan corporate culture created by consolidation, reengineering and delayering has been demoralizing not just for the staff but for customers as well. It would be wrong to believe that the massive consolidation in, for example, the banking industry in the US was necessarily a precursor to a culture of mass customization. The sense of alienation felt by many customers manifested itself in a renewed appetite for community banking. Two hundred new bank charters were issued in the US in 1997, the most since 1988 according to the Federal Reserve. The *Wall Street Journal* observed this phenomenon and commented 'These newcomers paint themselves as friendly, local alternatives to menacing out-of-state intruders. They woo customers distressed at losing their hometown bank, or dismayed by the impersonal veneer of banking by telephone and automated-teller machine'. One such community banking president captured the essence of the reaction to the counter revolution movement with the edict 'I don't want anyone ever to say "It's our policy". "Policy" is one of the weasel words of the disempowered employee. Policy is a craven substitute for saying no. It is a byword for bureaucracy. It tells customers that their requirements do not conform to the way that the bank does business. The very word "policy" implies a mindset of mass production'.[15]

There is a tendency to believe that the marketplace can accommodate both the mass production as well as the mass customization models of business. There is even strong evidence that within many organizations there is a belief that both strategies can be pursued simultaneously. This bifurcation of marketing strategy is deeply illogical since any endeavour to build up relationship equity by one marketing group is sure to be overwhelmed by the indiscriminate customer contact of the other. It is often difficult to discern, in these prototyping projects, any sense of purpose beyond the desire to experiment. The tendency for products to be customized in a world where some customers have lots of money and little time or patience and some customers have lots of time and little money raises the possibility for a secondary market tier to become established. This is the market for mass market cheap products where little investment is made in the information content of the consumer and this type of consumer will, typically, be serviced using kiosks, ATMs and other electronic interface environments.

The notion that this is the rebirth of the old class system is probably erroneous. The idea that some consumers will always value time and convenience and others will always value cheapness assumes a polarity that is wrong. The same consumers may demonstrate opposite reactions at different times and in different circumstances. Think of a train traveller who has the choice of a business coach with a reserved seat, fax services, Internet access and, on the other hand, coaches with standard service. A traveller going from A to a business engagement at B might well select the premier service because it satisfies his/her need at that time. With no need for these services on the return journey that same traveller might select the standard (cheaper) service. Old notions about 'first class' had to do with sociological phenomena rather than any notion of 'improved service' and passengers availing of 'first class' service were willing to pay a premium, not for any additional services, but for the satisfaction of ensuring that they would not have to mix with people of a lower social class. This pathology was satisfied simply by paying more for nothing extra on the safe assumption that only those sharing similar anxieties would do the same.

Airlines are increasingly challenged to explain why an extra two inches of legroom, a complimentary drink and a newspaper merits a charge that is four times greater than the cost of foregoing these pleasures which most rational travellers have calculated represent a trivial value. The fact that the business cabins of aircraft are still occupied indicates that irrational behaviour based on psychological phobias remains a potent factor in the behaviour of some consumers. But it is a diminishing affliction and the pressure now exists to design new consumer packages that genuinely merit premium payment. The actual business rules that arc applied by businesses to customers are often mind-boggling in their eccentricity. On one airline that espoused all of the trappings of relationship management it transpired, after a great deal of evasion, that the business rules that determined which passengers got upgraded related to how well-dressed they were. So much for recency, frequency, or monetary value! More interestingly, the airline was aghast that this finding would actually be recorded. The psychotic nature of the irrational enterprise is characterized by a mode of behaviour that is uncomfortable with being confronted with the stark logic of their business processes, but not so uncomfortable that they feel compelled to do anything about it.

Every analysis of the customer pyramid yields a validation of the Pareto 80/20 rule with 20% of customers generating 80% of the revenue. In fact, where costs are fairly allocated, what is generally found to be the case is that 80% of customers are not profitable at all and that the top 20% often generate close to 100% of profits. In the world of mass marketing, which is most of the marketing world, the bulk of the marketing budget is not devoted to these top customers or even to all customers but to non-customers.[16] Ultimately the organization that attempts to foster customer relationships must invest in the effort and this necessarily will starve the mammoth prospecting machine of the mass marketing organization that currently consumes the marketing budget. Any attempt to pursue both strategies will have the predictable effect of failing to nurture either approach sufficiently.

There is, in effect, a conscious short-term efficiency orientation in the enterprise that is laser focused on achieving operating efficiencies in order to maintain costs. By contrast, the business that directs its efforts toward the development of relationships is more focused on the longer-term benefits to be achieved by an effectiveness orientation. These are fundamentally different cultures and are, in many instances, now beginning to compete directly in the same markets. The chances that two separate linear trajectories (mass and personalized) can coexist are remote.

Conclusions

There have been many attempts over the years to increase the number of Ps that comprise the marketing mix from the existing four of product, price, place and promotion.[17] (These have, over the years, included possibilities such as packaging, people, probing, performance, process and power.) But, ultimately, this is a model where product is the overwhelmingly dominant component and it cannot be renovated in a world where product has given way to customer at the centre of the marketing universe. At the risk of minting yet another marketing mnemonic it is more relevant, in the customer-centred environment, to talk of the four Es of engaging (facilitating the customer to discover you), enabling (facilitating the customer to do business with you), exchanging (acquiring the transmitting information with the customer) and extending (developing the relationship with the customer to satisfy related and discovered needs).

Meeting people at the human interface is often cited as necessary to progress a relationship, but it should also be noted that the need for human interaction also serves to inhibit consumer behaviour. Remote is good when you can consume a service, cancel an account or move money and business at the touch of a button without having to endure the searching questions and agonized grimaces of another human being. The fear that compels many businesses to lock-in the customers will, in an increasingly depersonalized market, be brutally punished. But the depersonalization does not mean that the service cannot be customized for the individual; in a sense, the greater the depersonalization the greater will be the need to customize in order to reconstruct a relationship. The new marketplace is transparent, instantaneous, individual, mobile and volatile. In the past retailers analysed 'baskets', banks analysed 'accounts', telecommunications operators analysed 'lines', hotels analysed 'rooms', airlines analysed 'seats', insurers analysed 'policies' and utilities analysed 'meters'. The urgent challenge now for everyone is to acknowledge the existence of 'customers'.

But there has to be a real doubt as to whether the science of market-ing has reinvented itself convincingly in the face of these changes. The potency of marketing, as a force in the corporate enterprise, con-tinued to fade fast during the closing decades of the last century. This diminishing status, relative to the finance and manufacturing functions, was explained by Frederick Reichheld, the pioneer of customer loyalty measurement, in terms of a lack of clear focus. '[Marketing] has failed to keep pace with advances in other disciplines and has not defined for itself a meaningful and measurable role that is critical to the mission of the firm.'[18] While the measurement of customer retention has provided a real fillip to marketing professionals in the past decade, the design and control of the customer interaction continues to remain outside the remit of any integrated function in most business organizations.

The premise of customization and relationship marketing was that new technologies would enable customers to give feedback to the companies serving them. The resulting cumulative information would transform mass marketing into 'relationship' marketing. The technologies have arrived but relationships are maturing more slowly than the earlier adopters and proponents of the concept had anticipated. Investments have been made in operational systems that capture large volumes of data from daily customer interactions. However, few organizations are able to effectively use this data to drive their sales and marketing initiatives. The key to success is transforming customer data into business intelligence and that intelligence into higher profits. Notwithstanding the temporary counter movement, it seems clear that those businesses that have failed to (or declined to) reorient from products to customers are increasingly imperilled. It is undoubtedly important for a retailer selling wine to employ competent oenologists and it is useful for booksellers to employ enthusiastic bibliophiles. But customers are experts too. They know what wines they like to drink just as they know what kinds of books they like to read. In a universe of empowered customers there seems little doubt that the enterprise that knows its customers will outperform the business that is limited to product expertise.

In this respect two distinct meta-segments appear to be emerging. One segment comprises the cash-rich time-poor who demand convenience, multichannel access, self service, customization, added value services and time sensitive interactions. The other segment is made up of the time-rich cash-poor who will retain the traditional primary sensitivity to price. It is tempting to assume that this will result in a neat cleavage between customer-centred businesses focused on service quality and product-centred businesses focused on price. The problem with this scenario is that the cash-rich are not entirely insensitive to price and the premium that they are prepared to pay for the superior quality of service will never be more than a moderate percentage of the overall cost. For example, a business airline traveller is prepared to pay extra for a flexible ticket with certain service guarantees, but if a no-frills airline serves the same route at one fifth of the cost then the basic irrationality of paying five times more for the frills becomes intolerable even for the most cash-rich consumer. And a full service airline that is haemorrhaging customers to budget competitors can never hope to achieve the economies of scale that would allow them to compete with the low-cost business model. Therefore, we can state with some confidence that, outside of niche markets, cost will always remain the primary differentiator.

However, in examining the enduring primacy of cost as a factor of competition, we must choose between two different assumptions about how the market will develop. In one scenario the pursuit of lower costs through fundamental changes to the business model accompanied by refinement of business processes is perceived to be the only important task of management and customers only become the focus of attention during temporary periods of stagnation in the process innovation cycle. If we accept this assumption then the recent obsession with building customer profiles and relationships can be dismissed as a passing fashion. The alternative scenario is to assume that innovations in business models and processes are easily imitated and the tendency for cost structures to rapidly converge means that the enduring source of competitive advantage will decisively shift to customer service innovations that are based on complex information systems that are not easily replicated by competitors. If we follow the logic of this assumption we must conclude that a fundamental transformation is, in fact, taking place. To demonstrate why the transformation scenario is more credible we must first examine the nature and essence of customer information.

2
Achieving an Intelligence Capability

From Data to Knowledge

The Architecture of Information

Far from being impoverished most corporations exhibit signs of being
overwhelmed and engulfed in data. From this Niagara cascades the
conflicting, incomplete and fragmented reports that are the direct
historical legacy of the functional stove piping of operational information systems. This problem, the architectural miasma, is largely
the result of the piecemeal automation of various business processes
over four decades of computerization and was, to some considerable
extent, well signposted as a potential disaster by visionary software
thinkers in the 1980s.[1] Unfortunately these warnings were largely
ignored. Information systems are like buildings. Some are elegant,
functional, integrated and low maintenance. Others are jerry-built
amalgams of bits and pieces that have been added on in a haphazard
fashion. The latter more accurately characterizes early 21st century
corporate life despite the huge investment already made in business
intelligence systems. [Note: Technology is also a villain in the piece
because, for reasons too arcane to be explained in detail here, it is
still not possible to guarantee predictable levels of performance in

systems that seek to support a combined workload of high-volume transactions and complex queries.]

For many managers there is simply too much going on. As one report chases another in an endless round of fragmentary revelations, managers grow weary and frustrated. Today's truth seems to be contradicted by tomorrow's new insight. Quite often two contradictory truths are competing for attention at the same time. No one unified perspective is available and nobody seems able to assemble all of the fragments into a single picture. Decision makers suffer from sensory overload. In the fog of confusion decision makers do what they have always done when confronted by rapidly changing and poorly coordinated conditions. They look out for themselves. The whole ceases to have any meaning for the individual parts. The planning horizon of decision makers shrinks and they become strictly reactive. The more fragmented data that is introduced, the more confidence in planning decreases. This is the malign scenario that is playing out in many enterprises today. This is a classic example of a strategy based on 'bounded rationality' and reflects, if further evidence were needed, the isolated programmatic nature of the different divisions of the modern corporation. The information technology industry is still immature and informal and continues to produce innovations at a speed that does not permit the usual incubus of bureaucracy and regulation to fasten on to it. Rigorous methodological approaches to utilize new technologies usually appear in the terminal stages of the technology that gave rise to the effort.

There are a variety of ways in which information benefits an organization. An organization can have more customer information than its competitors; it can have better quality information; it can have better processed and packaged information; it can have more detailed information and it can have more timely information. The role of information as a driver of innovation has long been acknowledged and

Michael Porter[2] observed in *The Competitive Advantage of Nations* how striking it is that highly innovative firms are simply those who are 'looking in the right place'. Looking in the right place is rarely a result of intuition and, all too often, those who are looking in the right place are newcomers to an industry who are prepared to ignore the traditional norms and violate the established knowledge kernel. Looking in the right place usually means looking in a different place to your competitors and information is the navigation aid that guides the progressive firm to that 'right' location.

The power of information increases in proportion to the number of attributes of information that are stored about the subject. This is simply a variation of the network effect where the power of the network increases as the membership of the network grows. The greater the number of connections that can be made, the greater is the value of the total system.

If any decision in the enterprise is dependent on having all of the information in the enterprise at the disposal of each decision maker, then it stands to reason that no correct decision can be made by analysing parts of the enterprise in isolation. It further follows that each new decision that is made impacts on all future decisions that are considered by the business. Therefore, the challenge is to maintain in near real time a synchronized decision-making environment whereby any decision that is taken is consistent with all other decisions. The goal of any marketing system is nothing less than a complete description of the external universe. But there must be a point of reference, a starting point.

The fact that the myriad of planning, design, purchase, supply, production and sales decisions are synchronized merely means that the entire organization is in lockstep and moving in the same direction.

It does not mean, necessarily, that they are all heading in the right direction. At no time in history have we come closer to achieving the levels of efficiency that now obtain in most businesses. But much of management energy is canalized inwards, where operational, tactical and substrategic concerns dominate, rather than alerting themselves to the larger risks and opportunities lurking in the wider environment. The deployment of business intelligence systems that support the effectiveness of, rather than the efficiency of, the organization is still proving elusive. The necessary starting point has to be located in the planning process that looks outside at the customers of the business. It is the intelligence that is gathered concerning the external market that makes decision making effective and provides the basis for the configuration of all other systems in the enterprise.

Data, Information and Knowledge

In writing about the knowledge society Peter Drucker observed the following: 'By itself, specialist knowledge yields no performance. The surgeon is not effective unless there is a diagnosis, which, by and large, is not the surgeon's task and not even within the surgeons competence. Market researchers, by themselves, produce only data. To convert data into information, let alone make them effective in knowledge action, requires marketing people, sales people, production people and service people'.[3] This is a clear recognition that the conversion of data into knowledge is a value-adding process that increases in specialization as the process progresses. But this truth is not recognized universally. Many organizations exhaust themselves in the data-to-information stage of the process. When they fail to witness the expected benefits from the half completed task, they respond by abandoning the project amid much frustration and acrimony. Much of the early effort that was expended in the information wars could be characterized as the febrile pursuit of information without a clear vision of the link between the provision of information and its utilization by the business.

When we speak of poor data quality it is often understood only to mean inaccurate data, or missing data or inconsistent data. But very often the data failures of organizations have their roots in a failure to understand the value of data. For example, some insurance companies have a single transaction type to describe the cancellation of a policy. From an information perspective this has very little potential for exploitation. What is needed is a different transaction type to describe a policy that has lapsed, been surrendered at term, surrendered before term, not renewed or voluntarily cancelled. This data is rich in possibilities for exploitation and demonstrates yet again the persistent failure of organizations to consider the marketing potential of data that is generated internally. 'What was once a secret weapon for the rich and powerful has become a necessity for all business enterprises operating in the competitive global marketplace. As the world crosses the millennium, business intelligence will become a major force in commerce and government, and will substantively impact people's lives'.[4]

The reality of any investigation of a company's processes is that very few people in the company understand how they work. That is because the business rules are often unclear, unstated, subject to rapid and regular change, out of date or ignored. It is possible to interview a sample of key managers and find a disparate understanding of what is happening in any business process. Now ask what should be happening and dissonance levels go ballistic. It is often the case that those who most vehemently oppose rationalization, harmonization and regularization of business rules are often those individuals who have the most successful track record in such environments. They are useful in part because they flout the rules and it is their mediocre colleagues who often shelter under the umbrella of 'policy and standards'. This is a reflection on the imprecise, contradictory and irrational nature of corporate policies rather than a reflection on the need for policies per se. However, the advent of the Internet has ushered in a universe of comparable information and has forced the pace on defining a rational and consistent set of policies. In the absence of a human interface the hard sell and soft seduction sales techniques of the past, and the unearned margin that these techniques facilitated, have become redundant.

Information can best be understood as feedback from the environment. Every organism has developed receptors to collect data that can then be synthesized to produce useable information. As most organisms have more then one receptor gathering data, the act of integrating the data to create patterns that tell us something about our environment is one key indicator of intelligence. Another indicator is the ability of the organism to combine the data collected (and integrated) with historical data held in its memory bank. Not every reaction to the environment requires a process of collection, collation, integration and analysis. Some reactions are deeply ingrained in the hardwired evolutionary cortex and are executed rapidly in response to an instantly recognized pattern of events. Where we can understand how this process occurs we call it knowledge. When we cannot we call it instinct. The absence of intelligence has little to do with how data is captured and analysed. For example, most species of flora perceive environmental data, but we do not generally regard plant life as sentient. Often it is the death of the organism (i.e. when the organism discovers it is not viable) that is the first and last signal of trauma. Organizations that fail to distil data into information and knowledge experience a similar sudden demise.

Therefore, we can regard intelligence as the process that transforms raw data into information and knowledge as analysed information that is available to guide our actions. One of the difficulties with knowledge is that it needs to be constantly renewed by information; otherwise we experience that common phenomenon whereby we cling to beliefs that were once proved to be true but which have become dated and obsolete. So, we can conclude that information comprises atoms of data that, combined together and analysed, provide a basis for action. Therefore the connection that may be asserted is between inputs (data) and outputs (information). Knowledge is that information that has been internalized and provides the basis for all default responses.

Most actions in the business sphere (as in the personal sphere) are actions that respond to threat conditions or opportunity conditions in the environment. We see something that is desirable or available and we gravitate towards it. We see something that is dangerous or sinister and we gravitate away from it. Or the something that we see may be perceived as neutral to our wellbeing and we ignore it.

Over the past couple of decades the corporate organism has developed considerable resources to capture information concerning its own environment. But compared to even the simplest biological organisms this process of organizational receptors and synthesizers is incredibly primitive. But substantial advances are being made in organizational feedback mechanisms. The many questions the organization is encountering include 'what data is valid', 'what data is useful' and 'what data atoms are required to assemble into information'. This is proving harder than it might appear, but then biological organisms have had the benefit of millions of years of evolution while human organizations are a relatively recent phenomenon.

The distinctions presented here between data, information and knowledge may strike the reader as either unnecessarily pedantic or, alternatively, a glib oversimplification. But it is certain to be unavoidable in any implementation of a customer database that the distinction, at the very least, between data and information is made clear. For example, many firms have objected strenuously to the full disclosure of all customer data under the privacy laws of their jurisdiction on the grounds that they have vast volumes of data that: (a) has never been associated with individual customers, or (b) has never been recorded in a manner that makes it accessible to the firm or, (c) is not retained at all. This example makes explicit the distinction between data that is captured for the purposes of a given transaction or for audit purposes, but which is never integrated into a coherent record of customer behaviour, and information which is actionable by the enterprise and relatively easy to disclose to the regulator or consumer without incurring a great deal of cost. Indeed, it would advance the debate on privacy and storage a great deal if formal definitions of data, information and knowledge were to be agreed by the information industry.

This brings us to the question of what customer information is. The answer is not as simple as might appear and here again legislators have struggled to define customer information in a manner that meets with widespread agreement. Problems arise with distinctions not just between raw data and information, but between information submitted by the customer (name, address, credit card details, declared preferences), observations made concerning the customer that they are unaware of (e.g. consumption patterns), information that is derived about the customer (e.g. propensity scores for sales, loyalty, profitability), information inferred from demographic and other models, and information that originated from third parties (e.g. credit scores). The situation is further complicated by the fact that much of what we call customer information is not properly customer information at all. It is information that is linked to a device (e.g.

telephone, computer, credit card) which is a proxy for the customer but which may be used from time to time by a range of people other than the customer, thereby distorting any profile of the customer that is created.

Theory of Information

Claude Shannon was the first technologist to originate, in 1948, the concept of information theory[5] and he defined the components of message transfer that remain valid today. These include an information source (a database), a transmitter (a device to send the message), a channel (a network across which the message can be sent), a receiver (a device to receive the message) and a destination (the person for whom the message is intended). In addition, he introduced the important concept of 'noise' which is interference with the message or what we define today as data with missing or invalid values that is not useful or is potentially misleading. Furthermore Shannon defined information itself as 'that which reduces uncertainty'. Since certainty implies that there are no probabilities of which we are unaware, then, in mathematical terms, uncertainty can be measured with reference to the number of unknown probabilities that exist in our decision-making universe. Therefore, the greater the information that is contained in a message, the lower its randomness and hence the smaller its entropy (a measure of the disorder of a system). Therefore, uncertainty can be generally understood as the occurrence of an event that is inconsistent with the information that is available to us.

Using Shannon's definition we can assert that the value of the information content in a message is related to the probability that a certain message will occur. For example, if I receive a message that it is raining when I can look out of the window and plainly see that it is, in fact, raining, the information content of the message can be regarded as low. However, if I look out of the window and see that it is a sunny day and receive a message forecasting an imminent storm then the information content of the message is high. Bearing in mind the large volumes of noisy data that is expensively accumulating in most organizations as well as the banal conclusions that are frequently drawn from accurate data, Shannon's theory of information ought to have a much higher prominence than it does. It remains a useful principle to employ when considering the effectiveness of information systems generally.

Consider the proverbial fire in the theatre scenario. Where there is only one marked exit (and where that is the only available instruction) then everyone will rush towards that point. The outcome of that action may be wrong but it is predictable and at least certain. The patrons may be seized with blind panic, but are not exercised by the angst of decision making. Consider now a scenario where multiple information elements are available to the theatregoers: they know where the fire has originated, where a secondary fire has ignited, what the capacity of the marked exit is, the distance they are from the exit, the rate of progress of the fire, the destination of other exits that are not marked and the response time of the fire brigade. Now, a single decision is not certain and different groups will, in all likelihood, calculate different solutions. They may elect to follow a particular route, but they will not do so with a great deal of confidence. Information introduces responsibility. In this situation, not getting out of the theatre is not perceived as a matter of chance or fate but one of personal incompetence.

Now consider a scenario where the theatre is equipped with a sophisticated system that has been designed to consider, and dynamically reconsider in real time, all of the possible disaster scenarios. Each batch of patrons is issued with instructions according to their seat row numbers and if a clear and present danger occurs, they at least know that their best chance of survival is to follow the instructions that each group has received. In the case of data (one marked exit and no guidance) no decision choice is possible and in the case of knowledge (precise exit instructions) no decision choice is necessary. It is grappling with information that fills us with angst.

Information as Currency

It has been a truism of our times that information is power. Many commentators have begun to talk of information as an asset. In practice, though, information does not share all of the characteristics of an asset. For example, it is not absolutely necessary to proportionately increase the volume of information before expanding a business. In reality, information is more analogous to a currency. Information can be traded for a value. That value can decrease if it is made freely available. It can be polluted or debased. It can be devalued by crisis. Its real value is determined with reference to the strength of competitors' information. Sometimes, in extremis, it has to be withdrawn and reissued. And its real value is derived from confidence.

If information is debased or new information introduced without withdrawing old information from circulation we have the information equivalent of inflation. Where we increase the supply of information we do not necessarily get more competition, we simply force an increase in the quantity of information that all competing decision makers require to make a safe decision. History teaches us that when money was tied to the gold standard periods of major gold discoveries caused great inflations, such as the flow of gold from the New World into Spain in the sixteenth century. The past decade has witnessed a similar inflation in information where the volume of information needing to be processed has increased dramatically and the cost of decision making has been driven up for all participants in the market. It is only in the next stage of development that we will see an assessment taking place concerning the actual real value of information that is circulating in competing organizations. This will have radical consequences and will lead to the upgrading and down-grading of value in a market that, historically, has not differentiated information in this way.

The data warehouse tended to be successful at providing a strategic level view to guide business planning as well as delivering insights into key performance indicators for tactical-level decision making. What was rarely achieved was an operational level capability to trans-form the manner in which the business interacted with customers. The focus on providing ad hoc query capability rather then using the data to propel operational business processes was driven largely by the need to discover basic facts about the business in an envir-onment that was almost totally blind. But once the integrated view of the customer crystallized it was inevitable that progress would be made on segmenting the customers into discrete markets that would, in time, have the effect of radically transforming the business organization.

Cognitive Responses to Information

All too frequently our emotional responses overwhelm our rational ones and encourage us to ignore that which is novel, unwelcome or unpleasant. The following list[6] illustrates the top ten decision-making behaviours that are consistently irrational:

- People overweight new information at the expense of existing information. (This explains why, in the equity markets, stock prices continually overshoot in either direction as an item of new information is released – the 'pendulum effect'.)
- People are much more sensitive to negative than to positive stimuli. (Because we perceive threats more keenly than opportunities, the focus of many organizations is on their competitors rather than on the market.)
- People are naturally risk-averse and will generally choose a certain gain over a high probability of a superior return. (This explains the continuing success of low-yield investment products where the capital is guaranteed.)
- People arc, notwithstanding their risk-averse nature, much more sensitive to a loss than a cost even though both are merely accounting conventions describing the same thing. (This phenomenon explains why there is a tendency to hold on to loss making shares or poorly performing products in the hope that things will improve and that the loss will not have to be acknowledged or crystallized.)
- People recoil from the perceived risks associated with radical innovation on the grounds that it is safer to fail conventionally than to succeed unconventionally. (This explains why so many new innovations take a long time to penetrate the mainstream market and largely explains the phenomenon of 'momentum' in the financial markets.)
- People make decisions with assiduous reference to information that is available to them, even though they may be dimly aware that the information they have is woefully incomplete. (This tendency explains a high proportion of military disasters that have occurred throughout history.)

- People are capable of propounding contradictory principles to support different objectives in pursuit of the same goal. (A frequent occurrence of this phenomenon is the dissonance that exists between the strategic goals of organizations and the compensation systems designed to reward personnel. This reflects the ability of the mind to compartmentalize information gathered for different purposes without appearing to apprehend the contradictions.)
- People become by turns animated and paralysed by the flow of information where each new item of information displaces a previously held assumption. (This reflects the lack of a cognitive framework to integrate information and can be daily witnessed in the fluctuations of the world's stock markets as well as the succession of management fads that grip organizations.)
- People disparage attempts to engineer change in circumstances where no pain is being endured. (The 'if it isn't broke, don't fix it' principle has blindsided every organization that has been eclipsed by a new technology or business model.)
- People suffer from bias, prejudice and superstition. (History is replete with so many instances of these pathologies as to make any individual example unnecessary.)

People don't believe new information because they have not encountered it before. Something that sounds unlikely, or more usually something that sounds unwelcome, is frequently disparaged as unlikely and assumed to be noise in the system. The psychology of denial remains a key feature of organizations as well as of individuals. Flawed reactions to events do not happen nearly as often due to a scarcity of information as management science would have us believe. Peter Bernstein, in a historical review of risk and our reaction to it, observes 'the evidence ... reveals repeated patterns of irrationality, inconsistency, and incompetence in the ways that human beings arrive at decisions and choices when faced with uncertainty'.[7]

In retrospect, all major financial shocks, most notably the Wall Street Crash, were predictable but no consensus existed at the time. Neither, by and large, was the prolonged bear market that commenced in 2000 predicted. This was despite the availability of a plethora of evidence that included the technology bubble, depression in Asia, a global currency crisis and global credit crisis. Notwithstanding this mass of information the most prominent economic forecasters did not see the coming bust; they heard about it on the evening news, along with everyone else. This is not merely a case of being wise after the event. The reality of these examples is that psychological forces that we describe as 'sentiment', 'momentum' or just plain prejudice continue to trump rational decision making in a great many spheres of human activity. For example, many commentators have marvelled at the 'tequila effect' of a Mexican currency devaluation in 1994 that spread financial contagion across Latin America, or the 1997 devaluation of Thailand's currency that triggered a financial avalanche across Asia. These linkages were inexplicable because there were no significant trade relations between the countries that precipitated the crises and those affected by it. In other words, there was no information-based rationale for problems in Mexico to impact Argentina or events in Thailand to concern Indonesia. Paul Krugman, a very rational economist, has observed of these anomalies that 'it did not matter that these economies were only modestly linked in terms of physical flow of goods. They were linked in the minds of investors, who regarded the trouble of one economy as bad news about the others.[8] This merely serves to remind us that the age of information has done little to dispel the primitive anxieties and crude caricatures that inhabit the minds of decision makers.

These are disturbing signals of information repudiation in a supposed 'age of information' and suggest that homo sapiens is not entirely the rational animal that we imagine. This wilful turning away from hard evidence cannot be explained simply as a pathological optimism (in the case of the stock market bubble) or pathological pessimism (in the case of the Asian currency meltdown). Neither is it explained away by asserting that the future is always unknowable and subject to random unforeseen events, since all behaviour is explained at the time with reference to some information that is compatible with the behaviour being exhibited. It is this selective use of information that is disturbing and it implies, all too often, that information is tailored to suit an emotionally-driven momentum that is fuelled by a non-rational consensus about perceived threats and opportunities. When we consider corporate decision making as it relates specifically to intelligence concerning customers there are even more egregious examples of non-rational engagement with available information. These errors range from a failure to acknowledge those customers who are most profitable or loyal, to a failure to rationally segment the market, to failures of pricing, distribution and risk management.

This brings us to the uncertainty principle of information. As more and more information is progressively introduced in an attempt to better describe and understand the business environment the confidence in each successive discovery decreases in relation to the displacement of previous discoveries. For example, if we traditionally believed, for whatever reason, that product A is most profitable and then, from analysing data, discover that product B is actually more profitable, we are inclined to have an increased confidence in information. However, if we later receive more and better quality information and discover that product C is actually more profitable than B, then our confidence in the finding is diminished by the fact that our previous information-enabled discovery has now been proved wrong. In other words, if every time we improve the information environment and get a different answer to our question we begin to distrust the information environment. In these circumstances the more information we have the less confident we become. Contrast that with the certainty principle; that is, if you have very little information about a situation, but where that information is not contradicted then you can make a decision with a great deal of confidence, since the available information consistently points to one and only one course of action.

The reality is that instinct rather than fact continues to determine the cognitive model within which we seek to interpret the world. Information, though much lauded and increasingly influential, still remains an ancillary tool. In a world where information is scarce we are more dependent on instinct, and that sensibility is more highly developed. Our inherited cognitive model for decision making is based on the presumption of a great deal of ignorance. Because we do not know everything, or even many useful things, about the market, we fall back on instinct. In a world of incomplete information we proceed cautiously, backing a hunch, using the limited information at our disposal to eliminate routes known to be faulty, but without any secure knowledge concerning what path might be safe. The single underlying assumption about the market is that it is dominated by risk takers, i.e. those who proceed with incomplete information and strike out based on a hunch. Why else would there be risk?

In much the same way that financial investors adopt different approaches to stock-picking (ranging from value investing to momentum investing) it can be observed that different businesses use customer information in quite different ways to achieve a return on their technology investment. For example, Warren Buffett, the renowned value investor, is reported to not have a stock quote

machine in his office.[9] For Buffett, who places his faith in fundamental analysis, what happens in the market on a day-to-day basis
is inconsequential. This is in marked contrast to the legions of day
traders who eke out multiple tiny profits from short-term trading
activities. In the one case, the focus is on analysing information
for its strategic significance and in the other, the goal is to observe
short-term data fluctuations in search of tactical opportunities.
Short-term movements in the market are best exploited by those
who can determine what obsessions will take hold of the market
day by day and by correctly identifying what consensus will emerge
concerning these issues. The task of the longer term investor is to
filter out the noise and unmask the fundamental issues. Likewise,
there are firms that use their customer information capabilities
to fundamentally reengineer their business processes and reorient
their business strategies and there are other businesses who regard
the intelligence they maintain about their customers as a means of
launching opportunistic promotional campaigns from time to time.

But, in the experience of this author, most of those business intelligence projects that have failed belong to a third category, where no
conscious approach is being pursued at all. Most often this occurs
because of a curious faith that many business managers place in technology. This approach is akin to acquiring an investment trading system and hoping that the computer will make intelligent investment
decisions. Not having any conviction regarding how they wish to proceed, they flounder in an ocean of data, tentatively darting hither and
thither. 'Build it and they will come' is not an infallible approach to
change management. The problem with using information systems
projects to drive business innovation is that many businesses fail to
understand that having capabilities is not the same thing as having
a strategy.

Achieving a level of information unprecedented in the enterprise does not necessarily bring immediate enlightenment. Indeed the reverse is more often the case in the early stages of information exploitation. The automation of transaction systems resulted in more speedy execution of transactions at lower costs, but did not necessarily make those enterprises more information rich. The assembly of data concerning events in the business was often confusing, challenging and downright frustrating. The data hinted at gross inconsistencies and undermined cherished assumptions and had the effect of creating anxiety rather than satisfaction. Throughout the world the emergence of information heralded an environment of unease as facts became known that pointed at a trend without discovering it. In the UK the discovery that there were two times more social insurance numbers in circulation than there were insured persons was cause for disquiet. German tax authorities in search of tax evaders in the fast food business estimated the actual income of hot dog sales by correlating the hot dog stand owner's declared sales of sausages and bread with his mustard purchases! Information has become a source of intelligence, a means of benchmarking and a tool in the hands of a new breed of detective. Bringing data from diverse sources together releases intelligence which has the capacity to release latent value in the business. Like the imperial powers of old who rushed to be the first to find and lay claim to undiscovered continents the information enterprises of the moment are engaged in a headlong rush to be the first to discover trends that will place them at a significant distance from their competitors. Being first is, increasingly, the only worthwhile achievement.

Most investors are obsessed by market conditions precisely because information about this subject is widely debated and is continually broadcast by the media. What this tells us is that people use information that is available rather than information that is necessary for any given decision. More interestingly, it tells us that people have a pathological need to rationalize their decision-making process. This aversion to making decisions in the absence of information leads decision makers to relying on misleading or incomplete data rather than perceiving themselves to be in the grip of a psychotic episode. The natural desire by decision makers to be reassured that decisions are modulated by a rational framework rather than by random selection leads many decision makers into error. The existence of some information appears to provide that reassurance. But it is a trap.

Day-to-day decision making continues to be dogged by the continuing tension between deductive reasoning (working forward from known causes to effects) and inductive reasoning (working back from observable effects to determine causes). Since so many of the actions of businesses are driven by opportunities and threats, the dominance of inductive reasoning is explained by the fact that most businesses function by reacting to these events rather than proceeding from the general principles of an enduring business strategy. In other words, the mindset of business is essentially sceptical and reactive. By observing some phenomenon we tend to proceed from this particular case to formulate a general principle that guides our actions thereafter. The prize in the marketplace is claimed by the most observant business that accurately interprets the phenomena first. The fact that deductive reasoning in the determination of business strategy is rare may be attributable to the persistent failure of predictive models to distil effects from causes with any consistency. This, in turn, may help explain the lamentable state of strategic business planning generally. The absence of overarching strategy tends to lead to different (and sometimes contradictory) responses by different parts of the organization at different times as separate phenomena are observed and addressed. The absence of deducing an overall response to the market based on general principles leads, usually, to the atomization of strategic response.

Technology at the Crossroads

The knowledge economy of intellectual-capital producers is one that is not just open and competitive but entirely porous and global and is one where traditional manufacturing, (and many service), activities are relocated to other territories. In the increasingly 'weightless' environment[10] of the advanced economies, virtual producers employing highly paid knowledge workers operate in circumstances where the marginal cost of additional production is close to zero. Clearly, there are enormous advantages for an economy that has low energy consumption, low inventory levels, low levels of pollution, low financial capital costs and high margins on products. However, what holds true for the producers of technology is not necessarily true for consumers of technology and the absence of a productivity dividend at the level of corporate users has long been the subject of controversy. A variety of explanations have been forthcoming to explain this productivity deficit, including the fact that the qualitative improvements in corporate productivity are proving difficult to quantify and that information technology may still be too immature to have brought about the anticipated transformation. Cost justification has been particularly difficult in circumstances where it is hard to prove that there are thousands of potential prospects out there when one cannot currently see them; it is hard to prove there is fraud when one cannot currently detect it; it is hard to prove that costing activities are worthwhile when they are not, at present, costed; and it is notoriously difficult to prove the value of information that is not currently captured.

From a historical perspective, the BI marketplace has traditionally been focused on decision-support activities utilizing the technologies of data warehousing, query/reporting, multidimensional analysis, data mining and, more recently, information portals. This set of technology has served us well over the past decade and the BI market for tools and services was estimated at $12bn for 2001. BI has reduced risk and decision time in dealing with unconventional, unanticipated and messy business situations. Because of this success, the BI marketplace is under stress, forcefully driven in diverging directions by smart horizontal applications such as customer relationship management, innovative vertical solutions such as churn analysis in telecommunications and risk profiling in healthcare, and advanced technologies such as knowledge management and text mining. Some think that BI systems will be 'fragmented into little pieces and embedded in point applications, never to be seen by IT eyes again'.[11] The evidence supporting this view is widespread. Others pursue the mantra of integration and the logic of this position is compelling. But most are unclear as to how the dynamics for BI systems will unfold over the coming years and every corporation is struggling with issues of complexity, architecture, privacy, cost of ownership, justification, integration and application definition. Hence, there is a huge uncertainty within IT groups responsible for planning and implementing BI systems and within vendors that develop BI products and services. From this complexity and uncertainty must emerge a solution that has the merit of simplicity.

A data warehouse is a single integrated store of corporate and non-corporate data which provides the infrastructural basis for all informational applications in the enterprise.[12] The data warehouse tended to be successful at providing a strategic level view to guide business planning as well as delivering insights into key performance indicators for tactical-level decision making. What was rarely achieved was an operational level capability to transform the manner in which the business interacted with customers. The focus on providing ad hoc query capability rather then using the data to drive operational business processes was driven largely by the need to discover basic facts about the business in an environment that was almost totally blind. But once the integrated view of the customer crystallized it was inevitable that progress would be made on segmenting the customers into discrete markets that would, in time, have the effect of radically transforming the business organization.

The past decade has seen $80bn spent in software alone by companies who have been attempting to improve their business intelligence capability. In the same period the capability of systems to manage large data volumes has improved dramatically and have become more affordable for the mid tier of the market.[13] These investments have been directed at integrating data, cleansing data, storing data, analysing data, exploiting data and presenting data. Overwhelmingly, this investment has been focused on customer data and product data. Many, if not most, of the projects in this category came under the umbrella of marketing initiatives and a huge urgency has been evident in the rush to create the 'unified view of the customer' or some similar such goal. And what has been the outcome of this frenetic activity? Have most corporates achieved a unified perspective of the customer? Has customer loyalty increased? Have promotional campaigns become more customized and focused? Do customers feel more valued?

Many commentators, and not a few consumers, equate the information revolution with the Internet. This is not entirely unreasonable, but it is an excitement being generated by the mode of transport rather than the eventual destination of the passengers. What is truly sensational is not how data is being transmitted, but how it is being accumulated. Data surveillance of the transaction histories of billions of consumers on vast data warehouse systems presages the real revolution in the commercial life of businesses and consumers.

In much the same way that data warehousing was a solution to a technical rather than a business problem (i.e. the need to unify and standardize data) data mining did not originate with commercial applications in mind. In fact 'the commercial data miner employs a grab bag of techniques borrowed from statistics, computer science and artificial intelligence research'.[14] Data mining techniques developed from military, aerospace, metrology, census and geological exploration applications. The process of discovering knowledge in data has been defined as 'the non-trivial extraction of implicit, previously unknown and potentially useful knowledge from data'.[15] These artificial intelligence techniques, collectively referred to as data mining, are used to discover hidden patterns and relationships in data. Data mining is recognition of the fact that there are a lot of self-organizing forces in the shifting seas of consumer behaviour. It is also recognition of the scale of the task of information analysis. Human beings are competent to analyse small numbers of variables – eight is the upper limit that is recommended – but the number of customer variables that are now being stored number in the hundreds.

The more common data mining algorithms include neural networks (often used in predictive modelling to assess customer loyalty), clustering (used in customer segmentation to discover naturally occurring clusters of customers sharing the same attributes), association (extensively used by the retail industry to perform 'basket analysis'), decision-trees (used to isolate the primary benefits that a customer perceives in a transaction) and genetic algorithms (used to 'evolve' an optimum cluster of customers for a specific purpose such as cross-selling). While these techniques perform analyses that are too complex for the human brain, they are not a substitute for the creativity of the human actor in the business process. Data mining is another tool in the armoury of the business but it has proved to be no silver bullet for those seeking to bypass the onerous intellectual challenge of exploiting data. For the foreseeable future it will continue to be true that 'a computer can solve a simple puzzle, but no real problems'.[16] Historically, computer information accumulated halt-ingly in the enterprise, with each successive organizational function sponsoring and assembling its own information system. Thus it was that the artificial (and tenaciously defended) organizational bound-aries of the mid 20th century came to define the data architecture of the late 20th century company, where the sum of the parts in no way reflects the requirements of the whole. In the average large enterprise customer information is stored, on average, in 40 different systems, employee information in seven different systems and finan-cial information in as many as 20 different sources. To be sure, there were intellectual stalwarts in the IT industry, who pointed out in the 1980s that the tide of automation, instead of transforming the organ-isation, was actually generating a potential for unprecedented chaos. But, shielding their eyes from the intellectually challenging, (not to mention politically daunting), vision of 'the enterprise' information systems engineers kept their eyes firmly on the ground and rapidly proceeded to automate what already existed. Indeed, the standard information engineering methodologies of the IT professionals taught them to study existing business processes and align the software solu-tion with these decayed relics of the first industrial revolution. As time went on – or ran out – the possibilities for radically transforming business processes to simplify the enterprise were expounded, but the sunk investment of most enterprises in the legacy information systems that now ran the business made genuine reengineering a pro-hibitive undertaking. Which brings us, more or less, to the present.

Data integration is one of the most complex and far reaching of all business activities. It is the focal point of many seemingly conflict-ing interests. It is the means by which we can compare the inter-nal (cost-oriented) and external (revenue-oriented) environment. The quality of the end result achieved has a direct bearing on the business intelligence competency of the enterprise. This, in turn, determines whether the business can effectively assess risk and opportunity. Despite the enormous investments in integrating customer data (most notably in data warehouses) and the equally significant investments in campaign execution (most notably in call centres), the gap that separates these two capabilities has not been satisfactorily bridged. This is a curious deficiency and deserves some explanation. As data amasses in ever larger repositories questions are beginning to be asked concerning what alchemy we have extracted from it.

Achieving escape velocity of the data exploitation project is constrained by a range of factors ranging from activist intervention by mass marketing traditionalists to the technological and organizational complexity of the undertaking. The attractive notions of personalization and empowerment collide with the actual experience of customers which is often characterized by rigid standardization, alienation and unauthorized surveillance. The results of the investment are uneven and unproven in terms of business benefits for many enterprises. The reasons for the qualified nature of the success of business intelligence systems are well documented and include:

- **Architectural Focus**: Instead of constructing an integrated and standardized store of customer data many organizations constructed fragmented islands of analysis. Even those firms that made significant advances in integrating the information about the customer were set back arising from mergers and acquisitions which placed the goal of integration once more beyond the reach of the enterprise.
- **Business Focus**: In many instances such projects suffered from the absence of clear business problems. Many organizations proceeded on the basis that the achievement of data (and therefore customer) integration was a desirable end in itself. The marketing people were led to expect great advances when this was achieved. But how exactly it was going to transform the business was not always clear. Very often, it never became clear.

- **Operational Focus**: While the distinction between operational customer contact systems (call centres, sales force automation and contact management) and analytical customer intelligence systems (segmentation analysis, loyalty analysis and profitability analysis) are now reasonably well understood, however, the complete dependency of one on the other has been less well understood.
- **Consumer Focus**: While many companies have adopted customer intelligence systems and reported some degree of success, these have rarely been directly visible to the consumer in terms of improvements in service. As the willing participation of the customer is central to capturing the data needed for accurate profiling, the entire assumption of targeted messaging fails if the target is not engaged. This failure in 'visibility' of such systems to consumers has also been reflected by a certain degree of fatigue and cynicism in the trade press.

The relative failure of organizations to fully exploit the value of information has a number of reasons. One is the sheer volume of data that has been stored in retrieval systems in the past two decades. Another is the range of technical problems associated with the quality and fragmentation of that data. Yet another reason is the reluctance of management cultures to discard the proven techniques of mass marketing in favour of the unknown quantity of mass customization. All of these technical reasons are explored in more detail later in this book and most organizations are actively grappling with these challenges. The problem is not that management has turned its back on information as a source of competitive advantage, but that the process of exploiting information is proving unexpectedly complex, difficult, slow and expensive. Such evidence as exists suggests that most information-based competitive strategies that have emerged did not do so as top down initiatives, but were driven by the Herculean efforts of individuals in the middle of the corporate hierarchy.

One way of understanding the paucity of progress in this matter is in organizational terms. The main organizational handicap in the field of information exploitation is the absence of anyone solely responsible for the task. IT literature abounds with warnings about the need for a fusion of business and IT visions to make a BI project successful. There is no single competency responsible for exploiting data in most enterprises. Therefore, the political struggle of information visionaries is immense as they attempt to harness the commitment of the business executives (who must be prepared to adjust the culture of the organization), the business strategists (who must be prepared to adjust the objectives of the enterprise), the business management (who must adjust their attitude to data quality and consistency), as well as the IT management (who must be prepared to learn new technical and architectural skills). The compartmentalization of roles and competencies in the enterprise militate against any pan-corporate project and information is the most viscous of elements in the modern corporation.

Many commentators have peddled the idea of 'Build it and they will come'. In essence this view holds that data that is assembled will find a use. Or, to put it another way, that there is an inevitability about the usefulness of data that business managers cannot but comprehend once they have been exposed to it. Anyone who has observed the number of failed projects must have grave doubts that there is anything inevitable about it at all.

Information and Organization

Information is the corporate radar that is intended to alert the organization to opportunities and threats in the market space. Just as with airline radar, historical flight paths are no absolute guide as to where an aircraft might appear in the future. Corporate radar needs to be capable of anticipation. This is not achieved by information alone but by having intelligent hypotheses concerning what certain patterns of data might mean. Unfortunately, throughout the history of information technology there has been a disturbing level of dissonance between the business and technology functions. The information technologists understand the value of integrating data but not how to exploit it. Business management rarely understands the potential of information and are constrained in stating their requirements.

The trend of downsizing in the past decade has meant the evisceration of the middle management layers, which were the main source of analysis in the enterprise. Most downsized organizations find their operational capability and responsiveness improved as a result of downsizing. This is a welcome and predictable result of delayering since there are now fewer human relay switches in the organization and the information message can travel more quickly with less chance that the information signal gets weaker or distorted as it passes up and down through the layers. The obverse effect of delayering is that very little value gets added to the information signal in transit. It is very often the case that it is merely data that gets transmitted up and down the shortened chain with no means of integrating, validating or analysing the individual items of data. In other words, there is the risk that the data to information conversion process has not been conserved in the downsized organization and there is an evolutionary regression back to data fragmentation. In other words, these streamlined organizations are able to move faster but are no longer quite sure where it is that they are going. Much time is wasted in the febrile pursuit of information without clearly articulating the link between the provision of information and its utilization by the business. This tendency is exacerbated by the surprisingly few information subject matter experts within organizations (i.e. people who understand the business rules associated with information). As a result, the business organization becomes reliant on the information systems department to understand the meaning of information and these technical specialists are, very often, the only people in the organization who actually understand how the business operates. Matters are further complicated in many firms where they outsource many of the marketing functions, especially direct mail and telemarketing campaigns, to service bureaus.

We must now learn to understand the implications of these technological changes for the behaviour of customers and suppliers. What will define the great innovators will be the ability to truly understand how to exploit the business potential locked in the information. This is not trivial and it is estimated that, on average, the majority of relationship-based marketing strategies consist of at least six cross-functional applications, including database marketing, telephone call centres, marketing, direct-mail campaigns, field sales and Web self-service for customers.[17]

The single greatest barrier to mass customization within today's organizations lies not with the technology or the strategy, but rather with the organization's own inability to truly understand where the value lies. Relationship management has too often been used as an opportunity for one-way communication. Put more bluntly, cleverly targeted mailings and sophisticated profiling techniques may have helped the direct marketers to increase their response rates, but, used in isolation, they will not, and cannot, deliver true customer relationship management. I wrote in 1994 that:

> far too many organisations are focusing on relationship management simply to up-sell or cross-sell their products and services without giving enough thought as to how they will enhance their customer care strategy. By focusing exclusively on the sales opportunities that presented, they are ignoring other forms of interaction such as the analysis

of customer consumption patterns, levels of customer contact (including complaint procedures) and more effective analysis of customer profitability.[18]

This tendency to toy with aspects of a differentiated strategy while retaining a firm commitment to the principles of mass marketing remains an enduring feature of many organizations.

One reason for the information-induced paralysis has been the discovery by most enterprises that the quality of their data was abysmally bad. In circumstances where data was never analysed or used it tended to deteriorate in quality and much time was spent in addressing this obstacle to progress. A great deal of corporate data is decayed, intermingled and completely misunderstood by those using it. A 'law' of data quality has been developed that asserts that the quality of data is directly proportionate to the proximity of that data to a financial transaction.[19] It is rare to find that payroll data is polluted because of the feedback loop that is implicit in this kind of transaction. Customer contact data, on the other hand, is often a babble of inconsistent remarks describing different events and is completely inaccessible to any form of pattern analysis.

Another common cultural obstacle is the resistance of sales persons to hand over the human relationships that they manage to an automated supervising system. Traditionally, every new order achieved by the sales team was regarded as the non-replicable result of personal endeavour – 'the mysterious domain of talented individuals', if you will. Therefore, it is predictable that sales personnel will resist the introduction of systems that will drive sales on a systematic rather than on an intuitive or personal contact basis.

The attitude of many organizations towards grappling with customer information, has been to regard information as subject to 'diminishing returns'; the more information that is employed the less is gained from each additional increment. But experience suggests that, in reality, the customer information project hits the buffers of organizational inflexibility long before encountering diminishing returns on the information. In other words, the product centred organization has a limited capacity to make use of customer information and further benefits can only be obtained following a radical reengineering of business processes.

In general, the difficulty with the 'information product' is that it is hard to evaluate the benefit unless you have tried and used it. This is nowhere more evident than on the Internet where a huge volume of good quality information is available free, or on a free trial. The same is true for many software products that are 'given away' or offered as 'freeware' or 'shareware'. Two issues arise from this situation. First, how do you ensure that the customer actually pays for something that you have given to them for free. The second, more tendentious, issue for corporations is how do you justify the cost of building an information infrastructure in order to demonstrate a value that is not evident until after the investment has been made. This aspect of managing change has been repeatedly cited in surveys seeking to understand why organizations are failing to achieve mastery of their information.[20]

Two approaches have been tried, each with limited success, to address this conundrum. What may be termed the 'supply-side' proponents of information value tend to be visionary zealots who simply make an act of faith in the business value of information. 'Build it and they will come' is the mantra of this constituency and the information infrastructure gets constructed, often by stealth, by those who follow this route. The demand-side proponents, on the other hand, tend to be hard-nosed pragmatists who refuse to budge until a tangible business value can be proven in advance. Supply-side projects have occasionally been successful but are fraught with the risk of 'solution in search of a problem' syndrome. Equally common in 'supply-side' projects is the need to radically redesign the information product once users have gained awareness through using the initial prototype. Demand-side projects have had a far higher success rate when they actually get built. But a large number of demand-side projects stagnate in the absence of a working prototype and fall prey to 'analysis-paralysis' syndrome.

The question being posed here is whether we have to build the information infrastructure before we can build awareness of the value of subscribing to it? The recent history of targeted marketing has been characterized by reluctance. Technologically, it is no longer a supernormal challenge, but the impact on organizational culture is momentous. So momentous, in fact, that it would be foolish to think that any more than a modest proportion of the large global corporations will actually survive this transition intact.

The Value of Historical Data

It is an irritating habit of some academic commentators, when casting an eye on the world of business intelligence, to tartly observe that the past provides no guide to the future. As a philosophical observation it is indisputable. Probabilities based on the occurrence of past events can be mathematically disproved. But this is to miss the point of what is going on in business intelligence. Marketing is concerned with the recent past and the near future behaviour of human beings. And human beings are remarkably consistent in their behaviour over short periods. People who are price sensitive do not suddenly become more sensitive to aesthetics and, on occasions where this does occur, it is useful to know about it. Marketers are not inclined to draw conclusions about consumer behaviour next year as a result of studying the past century of consumer behaviour. The basis for maintaining recent history of customer behaviour rests on the assumption that this behaviour is not indiscriminate. Of course, academics know this full well; otherwise they would select for instruction students chosen at random instead of subjecting college entrants to well-established qualification criteria that have worked for them in the past.[21]

Nonetheless, a very fundamental question that needs to be posed about the enormous investments being made in decision-support systems concerns the practical value of historical data. Do management believe that recent behaviour of customers, markets, products, risks and channels are necessary to inform decision making in the near future. In this context the recent past and the near future typically comprises a continuum of less than a decade. The empirical evidence suggests that, overwhelmingly, they do believe this to be true as most organizations are committed to maintaining histories of customer behaviour for periods approaching five years, albeit with variations from industry to industry. That being the case, the next obvious question is: are they correct in this view? The contrarian's perspective asserts that, in a world where change is increasingly dramatic and markets increasingly turbulent, historical analysis is irrelevant or misleading. Consider what value might be gleaned by Microsoft from a historical analysis of PC usage in the past five years to inform their strategy for the next five years. Extremely limited would be the answer. If we reduce the timescale to two years and ask what value might be gleaned from studying the patterns of PC software usage in the past year to the anticipated usage in the next year, the value becomes quite high. But now let us take another industry entirely and pose the same question to the life insurance industry. Here the behaviour of customers over the past 20 years provides valuable insights into anticipated behaviour during the next 20. This occurs because the product has a stable half-life of 20 years in marked contrast to PC software which has a stable half-life of two years. Thus, we may assert a simple rule of thumb. The extent of historical data that is captured and maintained for analysis is directly proportionate to the accepted lifecycle of the product in its current form.

A young person taking out life insurance can be expected to be paying their premiums for the next several decades. Equally, it is possible to compute with reasonable accuracy the grocery consumption for the next several decades of a household with two adults in their late thirties, and two young children, enjoying a moderate income. More interestingly, it is possible to anticipate how their consumption patterns will alter and adjust during that period; as the young insured person becomes older, married, more affluent, less affluent, self employed and the older couple's children grow up and leave home. These become 'events' in the life of the customer that organisations need to become attuned to anticipating and responding to.

Of course, maintaining large swathes of historical data about customers has a limited benefit in a world where consumer tastes change rapidly, geodemographic factors are constantly altering and where lifestyle and fashion influences are more pervasive than ever before. But near-past customer behaviour provides compelling insights into near future behaviour and the purpose of maintaining information is not primarily directed at divining the future from the past, but at being able to immediately detect currents in the behaviour of the market.

Conclusions

At the dawn of the third millennium rational decision making is shaped by two factors – the abundance of raw data and the dearth of meaningful information. It is a dilemma that will necessarily engage the keenest intellects of the next decade and the most challenging aspect of this struggle is that technology as an ingredient in the solution promises to be of only limited value. Until recent times the technological advances in data capture and storage (and the economies associated with storing and processing that data) have far outstripped decision makers' ability to keep up with them. In the next phase, the role of technology will not be decisive. Generating more data faster is actually exacerbating the problem. Virtually all authoritative studies of information exploitation during the past decade have isolated the technology bias as a critical failure factor. More than 80% of all investment in exploiting customer information has been directed into technology and fewer than 5% of all firms achieve the full potential of their customer relationship initiatives.[22]

The next stage of development lies not in getting more data but in learning how to exploit it. In short, we have created an incredible weapon in the armoury of commercial competition and have, as yet, only the faintest idea how we are going to exploit it. Business thinkers and business leaders have grown complacent as technology crashed through the barrier of data scarcity. The next breakthrough of the technological juggernaut will be to replace the hopeless data fragmentation with an environment of data integration. This is happening slowly but surely across the industrialized world. But the next trick will be decisive – the art of data exploitation and the technologists are poorly equipped to assist in this arena. In short, technology is fast outrunning its lines of supply.

All technological innovations follow an S-shaped adoption curve with a gradual level of early deployment by the relatively few, followed by a steep acceleration representing the many and culminating in a levelling off as the final laggards trickle on board. In so far as customer information integration and management is concerned, it is clear that the dramatic growth stage is complete. However, the systematic exploitation of customer information is only just commencing as a separate, albeit closely coupled, phenomenon. The growth that has been experienced during the decade of business intelligence has been characterized by technology infrastructure rather than technology applications. It is not even clear at this stage if the applications market for customer information exploitation technology is vertically or horizontally oriented. The traditional purveyors of horizontal enterprise application technology (such as the market for enterprise resource planning systems) have dabbled with add-on customer relationship management solutions and the traditional vendors of specialized vertical solutions to the banking, telecommunications and retail sectors have also developed some partial customer relationship solutions. But the applications market has not experienced dramatic growth. Deriving real benefits from the information resource by businesses has been remarkably uneven. Where success has been achieved it has been typified by ad hoc initiatives and one-off successes, and individual enterprises have relied, for the most part, on their own ingenuity to figure out how the customer information that has been painstakingly amassed can be fully utilized. The conundrum that most organizations are now grappling with is that they have invested heavily in the customer information resource (typically a data warehouse) and equally heavily in customer interaction systems (typically a call centre). However, it is a very rickety bridge that links these two domains. Until real information and knowledge has been distilled from the data and is used to systematically drive the customer interaction process this will continue to remain the weak link. On the other hand, the distance to be travelled to complete a fully functioning customer management infrastructure is short. It is hard not to believe that we are, in fact, on the cusp of a significant breakthrough or that the few early adapters now emerging presage a new wave of technological innovation in what is, in fact, the second stage development of a double S curve. The first stage was operational; the second stage is analytical.

Whether two stages were inevitable is not clear. It is reasonable to ask why the intelligence element of the customer process could not have been coupled in lockstep to the operational element at all times. If probed rigorously it might seem that there was a chronic failure of systems integration which, in turn, seems attributable to a failure to surmount a straightforward workflow challenge. Nonetheless, it is clear that the complexity of fastening a customer profiling and customization capability to a fast moving and rapidly changing operational process overwhelmed most attempts to do so. And now that the efficiency gains have been realized, more sustained attention will be directed at the amassed customer data.

Many enterprises have remained non-belligerent in the information wars on the grounds that it is simply not possible to keep pace with developments. These enterprises are content to be responsive and to be positioned to take advantage of trends that become evident without running the risks associated with being early adopters. Risk is generally defined as the possibility of loss or injury and there is undoubtedly a risk associated with attempting to be first. However, we have also learned that the time it takes to align culture, strategy and organization with technology is considerably longer than the time it takes to deploy the technology. Therefore, the risk of procrastination is high.

Quality information is as scarce as ever. But what is more relevant is that where quality information is available, even abundant, it is frequently ignored. This is a perplexing issue and time and again in the past decade we have borne witness to great crises being created by a turning away from rational analysis and a resort to animal instincts. The herd instinct needs to be satisfied it seems, even at the expense of reasoned logic. The dot com mania or the Enron crisis may be the headline examples, but the real proof lies in the thousands of irrational business decisions taken daily by organizations that have the means to avoid them.

Somewhere deep within every human being there is a need to believe that competence is a product of an individual human intellect rather than the sterile output of a properly ordered mathematical model. All of the evidence, however, suggests that mankind will have to grapple with this crisis of identity soon.

3
The Eclipse of Mass Marketing

From Many to One

The Nature of Mass Customization

Stan Davis illustrated early on that the mass production system depended on low-cost standardized products being produced in circumstances of stable demand. And stability was enabled by long product lifecycles and a homogenous markct. Davis summed up the creed of mass production in the phrase 'efficiency through stability and control'.[1] The stability of the mass production feedback loop has now collapsed as it is constantly shocked by unanticipated input demands. But Davis also identified two problems that would threaten the mass customized enterprise. One was that consumers would be overwhelmed by choice. The second potential problem was that radical innovations in products can consolidate demand and swamp competitors with a superior economic value proposition, regardless of the level of variety and customization these competitors offer. In the current market environment the mass production model is disabled by the input shocks that Davis forecast but the mass customization model is also disabled by the complexity and economic issues that he anticipated. So, where do we go from here?

From a consumer perspective, mass customization is the recognition of the entitlement of every customer to be catered for on the basis of his or her own personal preferences and requirements. At its core this concept has the satisfaction of the individual's desire for recognition. From a supplier perspective, the drive towards customization is justified by the knowledge that mass marketing is a crude art form that broadcasts to the lowest common denominator in the market. Just as importantly, mass customization is the acknowledgement of the superior utility of a personalized approach to commerce, bearing in mind the assumption that there is no longer any technological impediment that makes the cost of personalization disproportionate to its benefits. Mass manufacturing of standard products communicated through mass marketing and distributed through one mass channel is now giving way to customized products communicated to small target groups and consumed through a variety of channels. The performance differences that are reported by businesses that have mastered the art of differentiated marketing are dramatic. Some surveys report 40% conversion rates compared to the 1–2% achieved by mass mailings of undifferentiated marketing content.[2] But it should also be observed that many other businesses have tried and failed to achieve these improvements.

The desire for individual recognition is perceived as a driver only in those Western liberal democracies where the individual consumer citizen is the atomic component of society and of the economy. In other societies, (most notably in Asia), the allegiance to group identity is assumed to retard the demand for individual recognition and the mass customization of consumer transactions.[3] However, this does not confine the concept to Western cultures where, in any event, progress towards one-to-one marketing has been slow. Where group identity is strong there is a definite advantage in abandoning mass marketing in favour of segmentation while recognizing, at the same time, that 'a segment of one' may not be a near-term goal.

The problem with market differentiation in general is that, like all management innovations, it requires the organization concerned to undergo a steep learning curve both in terms of the technological solution and the exploitation of the information the solution provides. Mass customization is a term which has been bandied about for years but the reality of current marketing programmes shows that rarely is the 'market segment of one' achieved. Where it has been successful has been in areas focusing exclusively on high levels of customer service and customer care – for instance hotel chains have moved away from segmenting their customer base at a high level, towards microsegments which allow them to understand individual customer needs. Hence their ability to assign you your preferred room type, complete with minibar stocked to your personal taste, before you have even checked in. Credit card companies are similarly able to identify risk at the individual level thereby allowing them to determine non-typical transaction behaviour and thus eliminate fraud. The customization model has also worked well in the build-to-order (BTO) environment pioneered by Dell with customized assembly of computer systems. The early adopters of data warehousing understood the power of customer information – and the benefits of the solutions to deliver that information. These same organizations are now reaping the rewards of true customer relationship management – simply by understanding what it is their customers want from them. What customization acknowledges is that it is not the product but the service component of the purchase transaction that has the greater influence on customer loyalty. In repeated US surveys of the motor car market dealer-driven criteria scored 85% as opposed to 15% for product driven criteria for repurchase loyalty.[4]

Today's consumers are an increasingly demanding breed. They demand that any interaction with their supplier be quick and efficient and are highly resentful of any transaction which is deemed to take up more time than it should. Some organizations have, at best, misunderstood, and, at worst, misused the interaction with their customers and have actually increased customer transaction time. For instance, the complexity of mobile phone calling plans has shown how the failure to use customer information properly can actually confuse and then alienate the customer.

There is a sense in which the drive towards mass customization is no more than a return to a more intimate form of customer service; an intimacy that was destroyed by earlier waves of computerization where automation systems refined and reduced transactions to the minimum level of complexity. In the process of this earlier wave of automation we created an alienated consumer who had no sense of intimacy with suppliers. The alienated consumer interacts with their banks via ATM machines with a limited range of options; the alienated consumer wondered what happened to the Italian red wine that they used to habitually purchase at the supermarket and which has inexplicably disappeared from the shelves; the alienated consumer dutifully completed the hotel registration form and provided the same information for the umpteenth time to the hotel chain; the alienated consumer purchased an answering machine that resulted in a massive increase in revenue for the telephone company (by increasing call completion rates) and never expected to be rewarded for this action. In short, the alienated consumer knew that there was no such thing as a relationship; that life consisted only of a series of isolated transaction events with anonymous organizations. And if there was no such thing as a relationship then it followed that there was no such thing as loyalty. The alienated consumers took their revenge on the anonymous corporations by being casually promiscuous. If they happened to encounter a better value proposition they availed of it. This level of customer churn was restrained by the inertia of most consumers who couldn't be bothered to make any effort to evaluate all of the competing value propositions available to them. As long as their supplier was in the same ballpark as competitors in terms of price and quality they tended to remain passively loyal. Corporations were reassured by this inertia and tended to use this behaviour as evidence that personalization technology was an unnecessary expense. The best example of this corporate complacency may be found in the financial services industry that traditionally preyed on lower income households who were seemingly impervious to exorbitant interest rates. The convention was that lower income groups asked only three questions: Can I get a loan? How much will you lend me? When can I have it? This is the culture of deference where consumers were cultured to believe that a tremendous favour had been bestowed on them simply because their mortgage application was approved.

The culture of consumer obsequiousness is coming to an end. This is happening because of increased consumer sophistication, more intensive competition and more pervasive information about choices, but it is happening most of all because of the early adopters of customization. Now that consumers have been exposed to the customization concept by a minority of suppliers they reason that if one supplier can offer this service, so can the others. What was passive resentment at mass marketing techniques is being transformed into active resentment. The early adopters of differentiated marketing are changing the rules in the marketplace and consumer exposure to genuine relationships with suppliers is conditioning them to question the value of remaining loyal to mass marketing organizations.

The Aristocratization of the Masses

The mass of the population that occupy the great middle of the bell curve do not just enjoy more homogenous levels of educational attainment, working conditions and income. They also enjoy the same range of labour and time saving devices, they consume more or less the same cultural resources and they enjoy a universally uniform level of care and courtesy. This is markedly different from the class delineated divisions of labour that were evident in the first half of the 20th century. This 'aristocratization' of the masses has, to a significant extent, been achieved by the mass marketing endeavours that gave rise to the consumer society that history will judge to have been a late stage of the last industrial revolution. The result has been a fundamental alteration in the social structure. This transition is what makes the continuation of mass marketing, as we have known it, inconceivable.

A false dichotomy lives in the minds of many business executives between services that are cheap and efficient (the perception of standardization) and services that are highly customized (the perception of luxury). This thinking belongs to the era of the first industrial revolution when mass production standardized goods were made available to the masses in contrast to the handcrafted luxury goods that were available to the elite. It is true that the choice was stark then. It is palpably inaccurate that this dichotomy holds true today.

Typical of the positive interpretation of customization is that of *Time* magazine when it was observed that online grocery shopping had 'restored some of the conveniences of yesteryear, when the local grocer knew his customers and their shopping preferences, offered helpful shopping recommendations and provided home delivery'.[5] There is some truth in this generalized characterization of the customization process, but it is also a potentially misleading reference point. There is an incipient tendency for personalization and customization to be used interchangeably. Take, for example, the hotel industry. In a typical hotel where the guest is a frequent customer the receptionist will be in a position to anticipate some of the needs of that customer. This is because the customer is a regular guest and information about their preferences is known. This is a good example of the concept of customization. Within the context of this example what is being described is the adaptation of what is essentially an industrial process, but it is a process that can be flexibly altered to suit the circumstances and preferences of guests. After all there is nothing fundamentally different about the core product or the consumers' appreciation of it. In virtually every hotel in an international chain there is a uniformity of architecture, design, cuisine and services. Contrast this with a hotel affiliated to the Relais & Chateaux group. Acceptance into this chain requires that the hotel be individually owned and it cannot have more than 100 rooms. These are hotels of character and charm and each one is unique in terms of architecture, design, cuisine and services. Any regular visitor to a specific Relais & Chateaux hotel will naturally assume that any special need they have is known to the proprietors. Therefore the service enjoyed may be described as highly personal. But the nature and quality of that personal service may not be uniform across all Relais & Chateaux hotels since no two hotels in the affiliation are the same. We associate personalization with the old-fashioned concept of luxury.

This comparison is interesting in some other important respects. For example, it begs the question whether, over time, the customization process will allow every consumer an opportunity to enjoy levels of service traditionally associated with 'luxury'. Or, put another way, what can 'luxury' personalized service encounters (as we currently understand the term) offer the consumer that distinguishes the quality of the service from customized service encounters? Charm and tradition aside, the difference between staying in a small 'luxury' hotel and staying at a 'standard' hotel where the processes are customized may become difficult to distinguish. And the premium paid by the consumer for personalization may become more and more difficult to justify. What information achieves for mass market suppliers of services is the ability to replicate personalization. The purveyors of personalized luxury services will argue that value is intrinsic but the hard commercial reality is that value is relative.

A bespoke tailor, jeweller or shoemaker will all produce a product that was commissioned, crafted for and intended only for a particular customer. In every case it will be a relatively expensive acquisition by a consumer. But if Levis can manufacture a customized item of clothing on demand or if the Holiday Inn can anticipate every need of a guest then the personalization that we associate with luxury is available to the masses.

What is true for services does not necessarily hold true for products. A hand-thrown porcelain plate will always have an intrinsic and aesthetic value that will distinguish it from an industrially-produced plate made in a mould. Similarly, a carefully crafted premium wine is a very different product from its mass produced pasteurized equivalent. But the distinction, primarily one of artistry and art crafted by an individual artist is, by definition, rare. In matters of art it is rarity that dictates value and the Age of Information is not any threat to this concept.

From Mass Marketing to Personalization

The market for relationship management software peaked in 2001 at around $10 billion[6] made for the year and includes investments in call centres, contact management systems, pipeline management systems, campaign management systems, click-stream analysis, segmentation and profiling, loyalty schemes and a plethora of other software systems counted under the umbrella of CRM. The figure for relationship management services peaked in 2000 at approximately \$20 billion for the year.[7] While there is some evidence of double counting in the measurement of the technology-oriented business intelligence market (See Chapter 2) and the more application-oriented relationship management market, these two investment categories are, by and large, discrete and separate. The investment momentum in relationship marketing slowed in the period 2002/2003 in the aftermath of the dot com implosion and the falloff in international economic growth, but a significant contributory factor also was the reported failure rate of 60%.[8] Just as with the complementary business intelligence market, the deployment of these new marketing systems resulted in a great deal of disappointment and frustration. At the time of writing, there is evidence of a resurgence of a more selective and better informed investment pattern that is particularly focused on customer profiling and segmentation.

The technique of mass marketing uses the same product, promotion and distribution for a very large group of consumers and assumes homogeneity in the marketplace. Just as the weapons of mass marketing are confined to crude area bombardments the intelligence required to direct such ordinance is necessarily also crude and approximate. Mass marketing does not necessarily assume that there is no contact with the customer but that all contacts are identical. Indeed the practice of direct marketing can and does live comfortably within the mass marketing framework. There are a number of different definitions of what constitutes direct marketing. The variation that is submitted to readers of this book is 'the process of directing marketing messages to individual customers'. This definition has the merit of being short, simple and indisputable. There is nothing about direct marketing, as it is defined or practised generally, that suggests that it is necessarily synonymous with targeted marketing. Very often direct marketing is nothing more than cold calling individual prospects or inserting mass marketing messages in individual customer envelopes. Targeted marketing is 'the process of crafting marketing messages to meet the needs of individual customers or groups of customers'. Targeting suggests that some element of analysis is being performed but the size of the target that is being aimed at (and the number of times that the target is hit) may vary widely. Individual, or one-to-one, marketing is simply 'the process of crafting individually customized messages to individual customers' and has been achieved to date by only an infinitesimally small number of businesses.

There is a seductive line of reasoning that suggests that there is an irresistible maturity continuum from mass marketing to direct marketing to targeted marketing to individual marketing. But this is not necessarily so. There is a clear cut-off point where the message being rendered has been subjected to a sufficient degree of personalization as to be useful, meaningful and relevant to the recipient. This may not necessarily be an individually crafted message. But it does have to be a message that the recipient values if only because of the feeling of confidence that any message emanating from the source has a high degree of relevance to them as individuals. And this requires a technological, organizational and cultural transformation that is not achieved by grafting on a customer-centred PR programme to what is essentially a mass marketing machine. Many businesses fool themselves into believing that they are making progress towards building customer relationships while steadfastly refusing to cross this chasm. But the distinction is, nonetheless, binary. Either the level of analysis being performed by the business can achieve a satisfactory degree of customization on a routine basis or it cannot. The critical issue is not the marketing technique that is employed but which of the two possible outcomes is achieved.

In primitive retailing all customers are anonymous and business is maintained on the basis of the price incentive. Intermediate retailing perceives the rewards offered by loyalty programs as sufficient incentive in itself to keep customers coming back. For more advanced retailers the rewards redeemed by the customer are seen as the price they pay for the information that they receive.

The Economies of Mass Customization

One common objection to mass customization is that the non-standardized business fails to achieve the economies of scale required to maintain competitiveness. Economies of scale are defined by Porter as 'declines in unit costs of a service as the absolute volume per period increases'.[9] In other words, the issue of economies of scale is directly related to capacity costs. The big assumption here is that the growth in capacity volume (i.e. production capability) and the increase in sales volume are both closely coupled within a single organization. What we know so far of the customer information wars is that this assumption is no longer sound and that there is a compelling logic to decouple these two separate core competencies. The physical integrated fixed-cost business is giving way to modular, variable-cost quasi-virtual organizations. For example, the flexibility available to an insurance broker to select products from a range of underwriters and customize an insurance package for a client is considerably greater than the options available to an insurance underwriter that has a fixed menu of risk-balanced products.

The real question is whether manufacturers, underwriters, publishers, transporters or network operators, can (or should) maintain any direct contact whatsoever with the end customer. For example, many traditional grocers have used customer information to diversify their business.[10] These retailers offer credit card, insurance, real estate, investments, personal lending and holiday packages to their customers. Of course, these are branded products that are provided by specialist financial services companies and, therefore, capacity can be increased, decreased or reconfigured at the whim of the retailers. In this world there will be only two kinds of business. The first type will be an exogenous business that grows by external accretion and is dedicated to owning the customer relationship. The second type will be an endogenous production organization that grows its capacity internally and does not own the end-customer relationship. There is also a perception that the former are in the business of pushing the latter further down the commercial food chain. But this may be an alarmist response to a structural change that is still not fully understood. After all, the skill set of producers is to provide cheap, safe, innovative products. And astute salesmen have always been adept at moving from one company to another in order, at all times, to be selling what their customers want to buy. The real challenge for information-driven retailers that are pursuing a multiproduct strategy to a range of customer segments will be to preserve the 'halo effect' of the brand that the diversified variety of services depends upon. The willingness of the customer to expand or maintain the range of products that they consume can be eroded by a poor service experience in any one product.[11]

In a retrospective commentary on his outstanding 1960 article, 'Marketing Myopia', Theodore Levitt observed that a number of bizarre things had happened in response to his manifesto. Among them was a 'marketing mania' that gripped organizations so that they became 'obsessively responsive to every fleeting whim of the customer. Mass production operations have been converted to approximations of job shops with cost and price consequences far exceeding the willingness of customers to buy the product'.[12] But this commentary seems to assume that customization of a value proposition is always predicated on customizing the product, which is not true. The manner in which customization is applied to a value proposition varies. In general, contract customization is applied to the terms and conditions governing the transaction and would typically include the price at which the product is sold to a particular customer or segment. Selection customization allows the customer to add optional extras to a basic value proposition in order to assemble a customized product. Design customization actually adapts or personalizes the product that is being consumed by the customer in a manner that is unique to that customer or segment.

Customer Loyalty

The idea of rewarding customers for loyalty and volume has a long history. The simple volume discount is a standard expectation of consumers. The idea of rewards in the form of accumulated points that can be exchanged for a gift or discount also has a long pedigree. The widespread usage of loyalty cards bears testament to consumers' historic willingness to be bribed for their loyalty. But the impact of increasing the rate of customer retention is quite dramatic. Consider, for example, a set of circumstances where two competing companies of the same size enjoy customer retention rates of 90% and 95% respectively. The company with the 5% advantage can expect to grow 50% larger than its competitor in a period of seven years. The key to measuring loyalty is to calculate, in addition to the net present value, the future value of the customer. This requires that the business understand the value of the customer over the full lifecycle of the business relationship. Writing in 1996, Frederick Reichheld (the pioneer of customer loyalty management) wrote 'today's bookkeeping systems, trapped in period accounting, completely fail to capture [loyalty] patterns.'[13] A majority of businesses are still trapped.

One of the misleading aspects of loyalty schemes lies in the core premise that a supplier of goods and services will reward customers who are consistently loyal. If this central premise, that suppliers reward loyalty, were correct, then we would witness a number of startling innovations in business. For example, it would suggest that suppliers would grant the largest discounts to their older customers who have patronized them for a lifetime, even though these customers are of little current or future value. It would also suggest that, if loyalty is to be rewarded over a long term period, then internal corporate remuneration and bonus payments would also reflect the long-term rather than the short-term value. The reader will know that we witness none of these policies in the consumer market and it is unlikely that we ever will. In general what is on offer is a value scheme that is disguised as a loyalty scheme. Take, for instance, the concept of customer lifetime value (CLTV) which is also sometimes referred to as the discounted future value of a customer. CLTV is defined as the expected value of profit to a business derived from customer relationships from the current time to some future point in time. It can be seen that this frequently used measure of the benefits of customer retention does not include past contributions to profit. Its purpose is not to reward historic loyalty but to segment future value. In practice it does not normally extend to the full lifetime of customers, as few enterprises plan for such long-term timescales – it is usually the case that 'lifetime' refers to a future period of three to seven years. CLTV is a measure that incorporates into one metric all of the elements that drive profitability. Usually the formula includes aspects of retention, cross-selling, credit risk, pricing and expense. It is also necessary to understand the transitions that occur in the biological lifespan of a customer that alters purchasing behaviour (e.g. employment, marriage, children, divorce, relocation and retirement). Organizations that achieve an understanding of customer value within the customer lifecycle tend to rapidly shift their focus from products to customers and develop considerable expertise in identifying what customers to attract (and what customers to relinquish).[14] Gaining this expertise means that loyalty drivers must be measured from a customer's perspective. And the key questions that a consumer asks when considering transferring their business relate to price, risk and image. Is it going to cost more? Might it be a hazard to me? Does it enhance/diminish me?

All too often 'loyalty' is perceived by management from an exclusively negative perspective. The behaviour that gets identified more often is 'disloyalty', which becomes a problem to be solved. The simplest way to address the problem is to 'buy' the loyalty of the customer by constructing a reward system. And so the customer who demands 'personalization' is armed with an encoded plastic card and the customer who yearns for a 'relationship' is consoled with the equivalent of a volume discount deal. Much of what made airline and hotel loyalty cards a big success was the fact that expensive business expenditure could be booked personally by the employee and redeemed by the individual or family member. Now this is not a corporate loyalty scheme as such; it is a dubiously ethical arrangement by a third party to transfer economic benefit from an employer to its employees. Indeed, the cost to employers of employee manipulation of airline and hotel selection is now well recognized.

'Churn' is the term commonly applied to negative loyalty (also known as customer turnover). While it is a phenomenon that is common in all competitive service markets, it was in the telecommunications industry that this measure was first identified as a survival factor. Two facts stand out in the market for mobile telecommunications. One is that churn is averaging at a whopping 40% globally. The second is that the cost of acquiring (or reacquiring) a customer is estimated to be as high as $400 in most advanced economies. Therefore it is of paramount importance for all businesses to ensure that, at the very least, the initial acquisition cost is recouped and, at best, that a critical mass of profitable loyal customers is maintained by the enterprise. While customer churn rates in the mobile telephone sector are spectacularly high, the more usual rate of customer defections is 10% annually. The important thing to observe is that the consumption-based highly competitive nature of the mobile telephony market is a better guide to future average churn levels across all sectors of the market.

The reasons for churn are many and varied and can range from price to quality of service, to customer care and to intangible factors such as the customer's perception of the supplier enterprise. Since in most cases of involuntary churn the customer is not electing to dispense with the service but to transfer their business to another operator, many of the critical factors are external to the enterprise. These external influences include competitors, regulators, distribution channels and strategic global partners. For most operators the task of uncloaking genuine intelligence from the invisible and fragmented data that is accumulated in product-centred stovepipes remains a real challenge.

Looking for a single explanation for churn is not practical and very often can lead to misleading conclusions. For example, many customers are disconnected or disqualified by a business operator for non-payment or unprofitability and this involuntary churn needs to be excluded from the analysis. Other customers may have been migrated by the business from a low value service to a higher value service. Other customers may emigrate or die. All of these instances of churn are benign and need to be excluded from any assessment of customer attrition. Indeed it has to be remembered that very many instances of customer disloyalty will not result in any voluntary cancellation event on the part of the customer – not every customer bangs the door when leaving. These instances can be identified only through an assessment of behaviour patterns that disclose the likely use of a competitor service. It is only from the totality of the data describing the customer profile and behaviour that sound conclusions can be drawn about the health of the business. Having reached a comprehensive understanding of the factors that influence customer loyalty does not necessarily provide a sound basis for business strategy. It is not until the measures of loyalty have been combined with measures of profitability and lifecycle that a complete picture emerges.

From Bricks and Mortar to Cyberspace Data

The greatness of the Internet is that it is a global collective, and this fact is peculiarly calculated to make it intolerant of regulatory incursions by governments. Now, in addition to this fact, which is general, there is the specific current attempt at control being exercised by successful 'portals', the gates to the kingdom that the user has selected to pass through regularly. Thus far, the full extent of e-commerce strategy has been to try to secure these gateways and entice the consumer onto an attractive hassle-free and monopolistic transit system. Why? Because you can then find out where they are going, how long they stay and what interests them. But there is no guarantee that, once they are safely delivered into the kingdom, they will wander off the radar screen of the portal owner and wander freely and anonymously where they please, or more likely, hop onto some other portal's radar. The definition of a portal is the subject of some controversy. The generally accepted and neutral definition of a portal is the consumer's chosen entrance to the world of the Web. This translates, in effect, to the selected home page of the user. This might mean the home page of the user's selected browser (e.g. Netscape or

Microsoft) or of the selected search engine (Yahoo!) or of the ISP (AOL or your local ISP) or most frequently used vendor (Amazon), for users who primarily use the Internet to engage in a specific activity it may be their favourite community home page. The theory is that if you can capture the user as they enter the Internet you can then influence (and track) where they go next. Debate rages concerning who will dominate the portals with distribution (the Telco operators) versus content (the Internet communities) and horizontal (AOL, Yahoo! *et al.*) versus vertical (Amazon *et al.*) commerce being the two most energetic debates. These debates seem synthetic to this author since the assumptions guiding current thinking are based on user behaviour that is erratic and exploratory. Ultimately this will not be the case as experienced users will lock on to a number of sites that serve their different needs for news, recreation, contact, financial services and commerce. The experienced user stops surfing and starts engaging. It is the destination, and not the entry point, of the user that will determine the utility of the technology and the loyalty of the wired population. The difference is that e-commerce elevates information to a higher value. Information is a prerequisite for inhabiting an e-commerce world. It is no longer a separate asset to be reviewed periodically. It is not even any longer fuel for turbo-charging the operations of the business. It now becomes intellectual capital without which a business cannot be established. Control of information, not passage, is the differentiator in the e-commerce wars.

The counter revolution addressed in Chapter 1 also extends to the Internet where many e-tailers have assiduously followed the mass marketing product-centred model. Just in case the customer is under any illusion that the communications from these e-tailers resembles anything like a human interaction the message: 'Please do not respond, since we cannot answer messages sent to this e-mail's return address' is prominently displayed at the end of system-generated e-mails. The message is very clear. It says: 'We issue instructions. You follow instructions'. Any business that can claim to be 'building relationships' within such environments is plainly delusional. Even in cyberspace many businesses remain intent on cherry-picking the standard customers and not straying away from the great centre of the bell curve.

For the past decade the bricks and mortar companies have been engaged in building data warehouse infrastructures to better understand the single integrated view of the customer. The critical issue that confronted the data warehouse project manager lies in the acquisition of the fragmented data (and the cleansing, synchronization and translation of that data) that is dispersed in the legacy systems across the enterprise. In the bright new world of e-business there are no legacy systems and it should be too early for even the most disorganized of dot com start-ups to have accumulated multiple diverse and non-integrated operational systems. In addition, the problem of identifying customers is effectively solved on the Internet without the need to employ loyalty cards or other cumbersome mechanisms that the bricks and mortar retailers have had to resort to. But the essential problem of assembling and exploiting the information remains.

Indeed, the need to differentiate web-based services from high-street services makes the personalization of the service more essential for e-business than for the traditional retailer. Another key influence, which is barely understood, is the psychology of the e-business customer that differs in certain fundamental aspects from the walk-in customer on the high street. In a sense the perspective of the customer could not be more different. On the high street the customer has an opportunity to make a visual and personal inspection of the supplier while remaining anonymous. In the cyber market the customer is preannounced but has no facility to make any rigorous inspection of the premises.

You can achieve monumental hit rates on your website, but unless you can demonstrate an ability to bring those same customers back again and again the asset value is questionable. The e-commerce measures of frequency (number of visits to website), intensity (number of pages viewed) and duration (time spent online) are interesting but they do not constitute real measures of a relationship. This is one of the key lessons that have been absorbed by the e-business sector. The lesson has now been learned and e-business ventures are now scrambling to acquire the business intelligence capabilities that will allow them to manage a sustainable customization strategy.

In the domain of e-business the assertion that customer information is rapidly assuming the character of capital rests chiefly on the following considerations:

- That, in the absence of face-to-face contact, the only means of establishing a relationship with customers is through the data generated by customers.
- Those e-businesses will be anchored to customers rather than products. Therefore, it follows that an intimate knowledge of customer behaviour is an essential prerequisite to any cross-selling/up-selling or customer retention strategy.
- That the e-business marketplace is a work in progress that requires the active participation of the consumers to complete and perfect the business model.
- That the psychological hurdle of gaining the confidence of customers in cyberspace can be achieved only through intensive investment in the personalization features of the vendor's portal.

But manning the portals and besieging the inhabitants is not a tenable permanent strategy. In the long run it is not the information per se but the capability to exploit it that will distinguish the victors from the also-rans.

E-commerce is characterized by dramatic changes in market coverage (i.e. globalization), an increasing tendency towards greater volatility in the market (i.e. greater competition and innovation) and a radical change in the structure of the value proposition (i.e. the possibility for one-to-one messaging). Taken together, these factors signal the end of the conventional retailing model and we have already seen dramatic evidence of the impacts of globalization and more intensive competition. It is also worth casting an eye over the endeavours of the bricks and mortar retailers, some of whom are forging ahead with ambitious loyalty card, e-tailing and one-to-one sales strategies. Others, who have been less than impressed by their forays into technology-led initiatives, are growing more cautious and, in some cases, actually abandoning technology-led initiatives. So it is timely to pose the question, 'will personalization be the exclusive preserve of the e-commerce market?'

Of course, not all e-commerce ventures have understood the issue of customer loyalty and have attributed value to things that really didn't matter, such as eyeballs, stickiness and unique visitors. It's like valuing a store based on how many people stop and look in the window, rather than on how many people come in and actually buy something. But the widespread carnage in the dot com world should not obscure the reality that many new players, with no history in the market, have emerged in the past five years to become the leading global vendors in a variety of segments including holidays, books, wines and events.

Of course, there are many exemplars of e-commerce firms that are pioneering the one-to-one marketing concept; Amazon, eBay and Yahoo! come immediately to mind. But for many other retailers the website is simply another place where customers can browse a catalogue and complete an order form. It is not just that the technology lends itself to one-to-one relationships but the absence of human interaction requires the substitution of human interaction with a highly personalized service experience. This psychological imperative cannot be over-stressed in the battle for customer loyalty on the Internet. In other words, the Internet shopping experience must be personalized in order to establish a relationship.

During the heyday of the dot com revolution it was clear that the prime movers in the industry were governed by a commitment to growth at all costs and by a carefully fostered belief that 'eyeballs' could be readily converted into revenue-generating customers. Events proved that it was not so. Since the launch of the first dot com it has been painfully apparent that they are continuously menaced by the promiscuity of customers whose loyalty does not outlast the curiosity phase. It is only human for many web surfers to presume that, like Potemkin's villages that provided a prosperous veneer to delude the Tsarina, behind the façade of the web page there might not be anything of substance at all. Combating this all-too-human, and often all-too-well-founded, scepticism is task number one for every e-tailer that encounters a new prospect. And the way to achieve the beginnings of a relationship is to begin a dialogue by messaging the customer. However, the ever sceptical browser/prospect/customer has already experienced the anodyne messaging that is mass advertising and so they need to be pleasantly surprised by receiving a message with relevance only for them. This is the essence of B2C marketing. It is the key to building e-relationships. And, it is substantively superior to the consumer's negative experience of alienation and mass marketing that characterized the world before the Internet.

One critical impact of the Web has been to divulge just how inflexible some businesses are. Insurance companies displaying their wares on the Web find themselves answering awkward questions abut why your *objets d'art* must be on a separate policy from your household contents when they patently *are* household contents. Utility companies have to explain on the online ordering form what precisely are the rules governing the payment of deposits. In the car showrooms the trade-in value of your old motor car might be a different value on each week of the year. In the face-to-face business model we had insurance agents who were expert in finessing and obfuscating when confronted by customer queries. Utility customers coming to a front office were simply evaluated for creditworthiness on a case by case basis without anyone having to divulge the rules, if there were any rules. And the car salesman was free to ignore price, terms or conditions and could haggle with the customer. In the absence of face-to-face contact you have to state the rules.

Consumers will recoil from non-disclosure by online retailers partly because any unanswered question will automatically deflect the consumer from a purchase, but also because familiarity with good practice in e-commerce is beginning to become ingrained in the consciousness of the consumer. It is the firm conviction of this author that much of the media commentary on the lamentable quality of web page design has less to do with the design features of the web page than it has with the incoherence of the business that is being described.

The imperative to clearly state the rules that govern the contract between the consumer and supplier does not imply that the rules have to be the same for all consumers. In most cases the rules are universal and the nature of this first generation of commercial applications on the Internet lends itself to transparency, simplicity and ease of use. But this is to undervalue the extraordinary opportunity that is presented by e-commerce to make each transaction unique for each consumer. With low barriers to entry, global reach, utter transparency of value proposition and ownership of every customer relationship, the Internet is as close as we have ever got to conditions of perfect competition.

There are also a variety of disadvantages to be considered which include the frustration of navigating the abysmal web page designs, the commercial bias of search engines, the absence of standards, the agony of virus attacks, the misery of SPAM, the invasion of privacy, the irritation of unwanted adverts, the affront of offensive material, the cost and global availability of broadband, the costs of continual upgrading, the concern about the financial security of transactions and the inability to effectively regulate the medium. Another obstacle to the convenience of the Internet is exception processing. The attractiveness of e-commerce depends on keeping the transaction costs low which, in turn, depends on discouraging consumers from engaging in non-standardized interactions. Therefore, when something goes wrong and the consumer is obliged to use the telephone or e-mail to contact the vendor, the result is often a sufficient deterrent from ever purchasing on the Internet again.

Of course, it must be assumed that these obstacles are temporary and will, over time, be resolved as more reliable, stable and rigorous processes mature. But, at the time of writing, it would be imprudent to assume that 'temporary' means that these issues will be satisfactorily resolved any time soon. Far from being a panacea for the time-starved consumer, all of these issues combine to make the Internet a medium only for those with an extraordinarily high threshold of tolerance. But the manifest advantages of the Internet also weigh in the balance and the result has not been a rejection of the medium but a retardation of its level of penetration into mainstream commerce. This has largely been to the benefit of the 'bricks and clicks' businesses that are not entirely dependent on the Internet channel but have successfully integrated it into a multichannel framework.

It is not just that the technology lends itself to one-to-one relationships, but the absence of human interaction requires its substitution with a highly personalized service experience. This psychological imperative cannot be overstressed in the battle for customer loyalty on the Internet. The customer is at the heart of the e-commerce business model and all communications are with individual customers, which is in stark contrast to the megaphone broadcasts that typify the mass advertising campaigns of the bricks and mortar world. Indeed it is a central characteristic of the conventional bricks and mortar enterprise that it is product-centred rather than customer-centred. For the majority of high street stores the customer who wanders in from the high street and makes a purchase remains anonymous, and the history of their purchasing and preference patterns remains unknown. This is not so in cyberspace where the customer reveals his/her identity in an explicit manner and where the customer's behaviour over time is captured and is available to be analysed. It follows logically that, if we are going to communicate with individuals rather than broadcast to a market, we need to have much richer knowledge about those individual prospects and customers. Acknowledging this reality, and constructing a business and technology infrastructure to capture and exploit customer data, is the first step in gaining an understanding of how to succeed in the world of cyber commerce. Oddly enough, many cyber enterprises appear to have failed to grasp this crucial concept as is evidenced by the proliferation of junk e-mail promotions that now augment the volume of junk paper mail with which consumers have to contend.

Conclusions

The space that separates the adherents of mass marketing and mass customization is broad and deep. There is no longer any middle ground. It is a philosophic battle for the heart and soul of the marketing department. For many mass marketing practitioners the aversion to information-inspired business strategies is encapsulated in the 'high-tech low-touch' mantra used to ward off information-based initiatives. The suggestion is that the replacement of the human interface with a machine interface will diminish the quality of relationships regardless of how knowledgeable the machine is about the customer. Not only is such analysis logically corrupt, since mass marketing is just as machine-driven as is differentiated marketing, but it has actually begun to gain some credibility through its constant misuse. A firm belief in uniformly low prices and high visibility distinguishes the mass marketer from the information warriors. Mass marketing fundamentalists are convinced that there exists some alchemy that converts visibility into sales. Because the obverse is certainly true – the absence of any visibility rarely results in any sales whatsoever – it appears any further reasoning on the issue is arrested.

But the advent of the Internet has placed the customer centre stage in business strategy. A critical success factor for a consciously customer-centred enterprise is to understand and anticipate customer behaviour. And, based on the conclusions that can be drawn from customer behaviour patterns, the cyber-enterprise must have the capacity to interact on a personalized basis with each customer individually. To date, the Internet has proven to be simply another channel to market and the 'pure' Internet companies have given way to the 'bricks and clicks' multichannel strategies of the established business sector. But it did not seem like that in the early days of e-commerce. In the heyday of the dot com mania it was widely proclaimed that cyber commerce would eliminate the world of physical commerce. It would not be possible; we were assured, to compete with the low-cost, high-convenience nature of the new medium. Never mind that there was not much convenience in purchasing an item of clothing that you could not see and feel; that would take two weeks to deliver; that it was absurdly costly to package and post the item to the customer who would, in all likelihood, not be at home during normal business hours to receive and sign for the package. There was absolutely nothing convenient about it. The blind optimism that suggested that infrastructures and economies of scale would emerge to validate this model was never realized. Only a very few of the dot com pioneers realized that they would have to develop new information infrastructures and capabilities to realize the potential of the new medium and these have, by and large, been the survivors. And the object of the new technological capabilities that would prove to work was personalization.

The conventional retailers, with their enormous accumulated knowledge of their markets were, in any event, never going to be vanquished with ease by the dot com upstarts. But had personalization, rather than convenience, been recognized as the key enabler, the course, if not the eventual outcome, of the battle for the online customer might have been very different. By targeting the physical universe rather than the philosophy of mass marketing this first foray was doomed to failure; a failure that would vaporize billions of invested dollars and temporarily grind the global economy to a halt. The fact remains that most of the participants in this offensive employed the techniques and value propositions of the last industrial revolution while having the weapons of new information revolution at their disposal. The first wave of e-commerce never achieved a proper breakthrough because it lacked a coherent strategy to exploit the technology. Rather it was the last spasm of an outmoded marketing mindset that was nearly to prove fatal to the success of the new medium.

Therefore, it would be a mistake to assume that history will repeat itself now that the second wave of assaults is underway. It would also be a mistake to assume that everyone is going to get it right second time around or that the two marketing philosophies are not still contending for dominance. All the evidence suggests that the assumptions and capabilities of the two camps vary a great deal and we can expect sharp winner–loser bifurcation in the outcomes.

4
Achieving Segmentation and Differentiation

From Fuzzy to Focused

Understanding Segments

Market segmentation is the process of partitioning the heterogeneous market into separate and distinct homogenous segments. A segment consists of a group of consumers that react in a similar way to a given set of marketing stimuli. The cost of segmentation increases disproportionately with the number of segments. This happens because as more and more segments are defined the distinctions between the segments become finer and the complexity of servicing these segments increases. Usually the enterprise defines a segmentation matrix and then, based on the data, allocates customers to segments. This *a priori* approach to segmentation defines, in advance, a framework or system that describes characteristics of customers or prospects based on information that is known about those individuals. The artificial intelligence approach allows for mathematical algorithms to discover customers who share common attributes without the subjective intervention of human guidance. The case for segmentation is straightforward. A business committed to segmentation builds its strategy on the basis of analysing customer data with a view to creating defined segments which will enjoy a differentiated treatment and thereby generate above-average returns for the business. And the key to earning above average returns is to understand risk in the market environment. For those who have sophisticated intelligence concerning the market a valuable opportunity is created. Business errors occur when bad opportunities are pursued or where risk is underestimated, or good opportunities are foregone where risk is over-estimated. Dominic Casserly, a partner at McKinsey & Co, observed of the retail financial sector in 1991 that 'more and more, the winning competitors know so much about the segments in the market that the new entrant or unskilled player must be prepared to incur major losses to break in'.[1] The ability to provide sophisticated segmentation techniques to the business enhances the ability of the enterprise to develop more tailored marketing programmes; to identify segments that are more important to the business; to identify segments that have been neglected and to become more attentive to previously unrecognized consumer needs.

Whilst this may seem a simple task, a typical marketing group will have constantly evolving definitions and overlapping segments that are determined by the needs of the moment. For example, a new campaign may require the rapid identification of a specific segment of customers to be targeted, regardless of whether the segment had been previously identified. The segmentation project is made more complex because customers may belong to multiple segments. For example, the same customer may be allocated to different segments of interest to the business, such as 'rural', 'moderately profitable', 'risk averse', 'middle-aged', 'late adopter'. As well as belonging to multiple segments a customer may, during the course of their relationship with the business, move from one segment to another. In addition, the segments themselves will be subject to revision and redefinition as they will be, in all probability, in a constant state of splitting, spawning and merging as the behaviour of customers and the external environment change over time. It is this complexity that overwhelms the conventional *a priori* approach to segmentation and presents an opportunity to utilize specialized data mining techniques such as clustering.

Just as the actions of citizens in civil society cannot always be predicted with reference to a single characteristic such as race, religion, sexual orientation, language preference, class or ideology, the behaviour of those citizens in a consumer role is similarly diverse. In some circumstances the consumer is price-sensitive. In other circumstances reliability is more important than price. Sometimes the aesthetic attributes of a product matter most. The task of understanding consumer behaviour is made immensely complex because the primacy of the decision driver alters with time and circumstance. Consumers may be price-sensitive to one kind of product and service-sensitive to another or exhibit both sensitivities to the same product in different situations. A necessary first step in assembling basic intelligence concerning the environment is to understand the basic building blocks that motivate the organism under observation, that is, the customers.

Stability of society in a democracy is no less dependent on having a comprehensive knowledge of how different overlapping segments of the population will react to particular events or circumstances. Any failure to study and understand the behaviour of (and interaction between) these segments will be damaging to the stability of civic institutions as much as it will be corrosive of trust in the business environment. Simply avoiding communications that are knowingly abrasive or offensive to a particular group is an extremely primitive acknowledgement of this reality. As the lifestyle, ethnic and behavioural mix grows ever more complex in society; a communications strategy based on devising a universal message to achieve a specific purpose is doomed to invisibility. Colouration of communication is the key to gaining attention.

Another key task in the segmentation of customers is to isolate those customers who comprise the early adapter group of consumers. These are customers who are less prone to risk-aversion and are strongly motivated to be in the vanguard of consumer trends. A similar segment comprises those customers who are disproportionately influential. In the online market in the US, for example, it is calculated that so-called 'e-fluentials' represent approximately 10% of the adult online population and that the views and opinions expressed by this group in online encounters is a decisive factor in the success of online businesses.[2]

In the past organizational change and innovation was driven by management, consultants, academics, competitors, suppliers and the vagaries of geopolitical conditions and the economic cycle. Generally, these were substantial adjustments applied at intervals. These changes will, most likely, continue to occur at intervals. But it is the fickle customer who is driving the blur of change that is the continuous condition of the market. Getting tapped into the minds of customers is fast becoming the survival issue for business. What makes the task complex is that customers are not, as they did in the past, behaving *en masse* with innovators and followers pursuing essentially the same trend at different speeds. What is happening is that the market is exploding into numerous microsegments that continually morph and merge into newer and smaller segments. There is no single truth to be discovered or new fashion to be anticipated and the single-minded pursuit of one particular trend is tantamount to abandoning the market in favour of a temporary ever-diminishing niche.

Any strategy that has as its aim to achieve a more intimate knowledge of customer behaviour must be underpinned by a system of customer segmentation. Of course, the ultimate goal for service industries is to achieve a customer segment of one (i.e. complete one-to-one marketing) but all mass marketing organizations will find that the first transition is from a single 'mass' to multiple 'segments'. Even the organization that achieves the nirvana of one-to-one marketing will find, in order to make sense of the unique patterns of each individual's behaviour, a framework that identifies shared characteristics and the emergence and decline of certain niches within the overall market. It should be observed here that the laudable goal of one-to-one mass customization has, for many businesses who attempted it in a single step, proven to be a trap.

The goal of business is to manage risk for reward. What is not readily understood is that many businesses cannot adequately measure either. Of course, risk and opportunity are two sides of the same coin since the ability to recognize and anticipate risk provides ample opportunity to take advantage of that intelligence. Businesses can hedge and immunize against risk and can, where they alone have identified the risk, realize substantial rewards in the market. Managing risk effectively determines overall performances since overestimates of risk needlessly retard growth and underestimates of risk are potentially catastrophic. Having the capability to confidently measure risk provides the basis for optimized performance. Key to any successful risk management strategy is the avoidance of concentrated risk in any market or segment of the business.

Market Segments or Customer Segments?

It is often the case that market niches (i.e. modestly-sized groups of customers exhibiting similar behaviour that is different and distinct from the mainstream market) are confused with market segments of the mainstream market. Those firms that serve the consumer market are ordinarily divided into categories such as fast moving consumer goods (e.g. food and beverage), durables (e.g. cars) or services (e.g. banks). These are sometimes referred to as segments when it is more proper to regard them as markets. There has also been a historical tendency to regard customer segments as separate markets. Therefore a telephone company might regard its business as addressing the residential and business 'segments' or a retail bookseller might distinguish between its fiction and non-fiction 'segments'. But this is an imprecise use of the term since these are, in effect, different markets or at best 'meta segments' of a market. It would be extremely helpful if we could define market segmentation as 'the process of identifying customers who comprise a homogenous group of consumers for a specific range of goods and services' and customer segmentation as the 'differentiation of customers within a defined market'.

For example, restaurants cater to people who wish to eat. The people who may turn up will include people requiring a leisurely romantic meal, people in a hurry, smokers, non-smokers, vegetarians, disabled people, elderly people with special needs, parents with infants, people who prefer Asian food, Italian food and so on. Now which of these categorizations describe markets, which are niche markets and which are actually customer segments of a market? Clearly it would be possible to have a restaurant serving Asian food, including vegetarian options, that catered to smokers and non-smokers (local legislation allowing), that had a kiddies menu and that facilitated wheelchair access. These are undoubtedly different customer segments of interest to a restaurateur who could conceivably cater to all of these segments. The relationship between the market (i.e. an Asian food restaurant) and the individual segments catered to is clear. But it would be very odd to encounter a restaurant that served Chinese and Italian food and catered for people in a hurry as well as those seeking a romantic night out. There is a market for Chinese restaurants just as there is a market for Italian restaurants. There is also a market for fast food restaurants, just as there is a market for restaurants with a good wine list serving a leisurely five-course meal. Likewise, a restaurant without a wine list serving only vegetarian food to non-smoking adults would (at the time of writing) be regarded as a niche market even though it may be more tightly defined than many segments of a mainstream market. The product and service requirements of customers determine markets and markets are defined by the value proposition that is published. It is within these markets that customer segmentation occurs.

Among the information warriors, and in particular in the electronic commerce arena, the approach to segmentation is very different since they realize that customers take no notice of how companies segment their market. Neither is the customer aware or interested if they are being treated individually or as part of a segment. The customer is only interested in deciding which business meets their needs most exactly and is most responsive to their individual requirements. Therefore, the customer-centred approach is much more concerned with the preferences, sensitivities, permissions, values, behaviour, attitudes and opinions of the customers under scrutiny. It is, therefore, a much more information-intensive process, with different inputs and outputs to the product-centred approach.

In the one case we have the familiar product-led approach where segmentation is driven by the need to find customers who match the requirements of the product. This method of segmentation is not especially information intensive as it simply involves passing a slide rule over each customer to establish if they represent a match. In using this approach the goal is to distinguish those customers who have the same or similar requirements which can be satisfied by a distinct marketing mix. The marketing mix is the core formula of the mass marketing philosophy and refers to the 4 Ps of product (features), price (value), place (availability) and promotion (publicity). Established in the 1950s by E. Jerome McCarthy the marketing mix was defined as 'the controllable variables that an organization can coordinate to satisfy the target market'. While minor variations may be made over time to the fixed value proposition represented by the marketing mix it will, at all times, remain a fixed value proposition, or range of value propositions, in search of customers who meet the value proposition criteria. The intelligence gleaned from segmentation does provide an input to adapting the value propositions on offer but the assumption is that all customers who are allocated to a defined market will be treated in the same way. It is for this reason that this method is often referred to as market segmentation rather than customer segmentation and these two terms represent a useful means of distinguishing between the two concepts. Therefore, it is essential to emphasize that customer placement in a genuine customer segmentation model is determined by customer profile and behaviour; customer segments do not exist to satisfy the convenience or exigencies of the business. In the product-centred universe that many businesses still inhabit it is customary for customers to be chopped and desiccated into tablets that can be processed and digested easily by the business. In this environment all non-standard shapes are rejected in the relentless pursuit of customers who meet the specification of the product. However, since the advocates of mass marketing are largely non-belligerent in the information wars there is little point in detaining the reader further on the merits of this approach.

Among the information warriors, and in particular in the electronic commerce arena, the approach to segmentation is very different since these businesses are more likely to diversify their products and services to meet the needs of their customers rather than continually replacing their customers with new ones as existing customers fail to meet the exacting requirements of the narrow product focus. For these businesses what is important is to own the customer relationship and to leverage that relationship to its fullest extent. When the question 'what are your core competencies?' is posed to such businesses the answer is never expressed in terms of a product orientation or even in terms of a high-level abstraction such as 'retailing'. The answer is always that their core competency is exploiting customer information. It is very likely that the way these businesses will evolve will be to delegate or subcontract the actual delivery of services to product-centred specialist businesses that will never own the customer relationship and, consequently, are fated to live further down the economic food chain in the new commercial landscape.

The test of a business that has genuinely embraced genuine customer, as opposed to market, segmentation is whether the focus of the business has moved from product to customer. In the traditional business model the critical issue was if the product (which was perceived as tangible and stable) could be sold to customers (who were perceived to be spectral and fickle). When an enterprise invests time, money and resources in understanding customer behaviour, it quickly becomes apparent that the customer is a far more stable anchor for the business than are products.

Therefore, the customer-centred approach is much more concerned with the preferences, sensitivities, permissions, values, behaviour, attitudes and opinions of the customers under scrutiny. It is, therefore, a much more information-intensive process, with different inputs and outputs to the product-centred approach.

Segmentation in the Post-Industrial Society

The wider sociopolitical landscape is altering in ways not seen since the industrial revolution of the 18th century. Just as that industrial revolution witnessed the move from physical property to financial capital as a measure of economic value we have witnessed in the past decade a shift from financial capital to human talent as the locus of value. Capital now chases intellectual property which is a term we use to describe knowledge. Technology is altering human potential as we move from a world of chance (where we live, whether we can have children, what we can purchase, whether we are bald) to a world of choice. It would be peculiar if these changes were not reflected in a fundamentally altered stratification of the societies that we inhabit. Two areas, in particular, have emerged strongly in the past decade as fruitful areas of research. One is geodemographic analysis; the other lifestyle analysis.

Geodemographics is the study of the association between location and demographic profile and the pioneering work in this field was first produced in the United States but is now commonplace in most advanced countries.[3] Geodemographic profiles are based on census data and there is an increasing tendency to blend the census data with lifestyle data available from other sources to create powerful new marketing tools. As with all forms of segmentation, systematic geodemographic profiling is a relatively new discipline and one leading expert has observed that 'it has long been acknowledged that the development of small area geodemographic discriminators is rather more of an art than science, involving a number of key choices in the course of typology development – including the number and specification of variables, the number of clusters sought, the form of clustering algorithm to be employed, among others'.[4] Nonetheless, the mathematical probability that correct assumptions are being made about the residents of a particular postcode is increasing all the time.

There are many drivers of segmentation arising in the broader socio-economic and political landscape. The social model of the industrial society that survived in most Western countries until the 1970s was largely hierarchical and conformed to a classic pyramid structure. At the top were a small number of the economic and social elite, followed by larger numbers from the professional and managerial sector, followed by larger numbers of white collar clerical workers and the base of the pyramid was occupied by the masses of skilled, semi-skilled and unskilled manual workers.

The post-industrial society is very different and is better characterized by a classic bell curve shape representing the two economic extremes at each end but with the vast majority of the population concentrated in the centre. This, the 'great middle', is the target for virtually all mainstream businesses. Differences between manual and clerical work have dissolved with the increasing similarity of the automated office and factory environments. What is increasingly referred to as the 'contented class' or the 'two-thirds society'[5] accounts for 70–80% of the population of most modern economies. Educational attainment has seen post-second level participation in education rise from a meagre 10% in 1975 to levels above 70% in many advanced countries today. But increasing economic and cultural convergence does not necessarily imply consumer homogeneity. Progress has also been made in eliminating a wide range of previously existing social prejudices and pathologies which has, in turn, validated a diverse and variegated range of distinct behaviours, values, lifestyles, attitudes and patterns of consumption. Psychographics is replacing demographics as the key to uncloaking segments within economies and in the global market. Globalization demands conformity with a subset of economic, legal, technological and linguistic standards that will evolve as the common property of the global community. The process of globalization as a new world order differs significantly from the imperialist models that preceded it in so far as it does not demand social conformity with an imposed social order. It may be that some degree of social and cultural standardization may emerge voluntarily over time, but any attempt to impose it will wreck the globalization project. Understanding difference will be a key differentiator for those businesses wishing to thrive on a global stage.

What are the Measures of Segmentation?

The direct marketing sector has, historically, been driven by the three key measures of recency, frequency and monetary value, commonly known by the acronym 'RFM'. (These measures are also sometimes referred to as CAR indicators where CAR represents cash, additionality and recency, essentially the same values as RFM.) On the other hand, the conventional relationship management wisdom is based on measures of loyalty, latency and lifetime value. Clearly, these two approaches are in conflict since the RFM premise rests on the assumption that profitability derives from large transactions (that are recent or frequent or both) while the relationship management goal is to ensure that the business gains a customer's entire category spend and maintains that relationship over time. These competing strategies simply reflect the reality that the consumer is apprehended in different ways by different businesses.

Mass marketing is concerned to discover the mean average of the market (which is theoretical and does not ever exist as an actual customer). By contrast, the pursuit of segments is concerned with the discovery of modal averages which are those customers who represent the largest concentrations (which are real and do exist as actual customers). This is not to suggest that mass marketing techniques do not recognize segments; but all too often the practice of mass marketing is not to discover segments, but instead to use advertising to mould and create them.

As precision delivery capability has grown ever more sophisticated, target selection intelligence remains primitive. While the benefits of segmentation are readily acknowledged, as is the complexity of the undertaking, there is a steep learning curve for most organizations to achieve competence in this activity. Despite the fact that segmentation is one of the most fundamental concepts in marketing *CIO Magazine* declared in 2000 that 'analysts and practitioners in the marketing departments of the Fortune 1000 view customer segmentation as a great way to reach consumers, but few companies do it effectively or can boast much success'.[6] Many organizations have understood the need for the customization of marketing, in all its forms, so that a business enterprise can develop closer and more personalized relationships with its customers. And this understanding has led, quite naturally, to an immediate requirement for the business to break down its total customer base into distinct segments, each of which warrants its own unique marketing approach. Customer segmentation is the process of partitioning a heterogeneous market into separate and distinct homogenous segments. Once a market has been segmented, further analysis can reveal interesting patterns within individual segments, and it may then prove profitable to conduct further segmentation processes on the individual segments that resulted from the initial segmentation process.

Effective segmentation requires a balance to be struck between knowing what to sell to certain segments (behaviour profile), how to sell to those segments (attitudes and opinions profile), where to sell to them (geographic and channel profile) and when to sell to those segments (lifecycle profile). The difficulty in defining the segmentation requirements of the marketing function is complicated, as always, by the inflexible organizational stovepipes of function and complex lattice of processes. What seem like the most critical measures varies from one organizational function to another as they perceive threats and opportunities from the constrained view of their own porthole.

Technical Approaches to Customer Segmentation

Marketing executives who have dipped into the literature of segmentation analysis tend to become transfixed by the table of contents. It is little wonder that they blanch at items such as 'An Exploration of the Application of Dynamic Concomitant Variable Mixture Regression Models' or recoil from offering an opinion on whether consumer preference variables are 'distributed over the global population according to a unimodal distribution or according to a discrete distribution across homogenous segments'. However, in circumstances where many businesses cannot distinguish between loyal and disloyal customers they ought not to be too concerned about the more advanced application of these techniques.

There are two fundamentally distinct approaches to segmentation. The first involves the marketing professional in defining a framework for the segmentation that is based on known characteristics of customers. This is called *a priori* segmentation, and reflects the way most marketing professionals instinctively think about their work.

When they try to make sense of their market through analysis, they tend to base the analysis on existing characteristics of the business (such as existing products, channels, accounts), or on fixed geographic boundaries (such as country, county, city), or on demographic data (such as age, gender, income) or existing profitability levels (such as high, medium, low).

Using such characteristics as the basis for segmentation can yield valuable and usually readily understandable results. But *a priori* segmentation is constrained by the extent to which the marketing professional already understands the business's market and the degree of invention and insight the marketing professional can bring to bear on the definition of the framework that determines the subsets into which customers are placed. It can also prove arbitrary, synthetic and potentially misleading.

The second principal approach to segmentation employs a clustering algorithm to discover naturally occurring clusters of customers who share common characteristics or behave in the same way. This is called cluster segmentation, and can be a way of discovering interesting patterns that are marbled through segments defined under the *a priori* method. Cluster segmentation leads to the discovery of all kinds of clusters of different sizes and shapes that would be unlikely to result from a framework defined under *a priori* segmentation. Cluster segmentation can also discover customers who belong to no cluster and who have needs and behaviours that are inconsistent with the overwhelming majority of customers. This is crucial intelligence for the business.

It is normal to use a combination of *a priori* and cluster segmentation. For example, using *a priori* segmentation for an initial segmentation effort in the new-car market, might involve use of a combination of demographic, socioeconomic, geographic, personality, lifestyle and behavioural characteristics. The results would, within the context set by this choice of customer attributes, provide an effective basis for designing a series of sales campaigns aimed at up-selling and cross-selling.

But this should not be regarded as the end of the segmentation exercise. A cluster analysis of one or more of the segments produced by the *a priori* method very often yields further insight, which may result in refinement (or even substantial modification) of the initial conclusions, or may suggest new and important marketing opportunities.

Cluster analysis can result in the discovery of a small but highly valuable cluster of people of high potential value who have needs that are quite different from the needs of other people with whom they originally shared a segment under an initial *a priori* analysis.

To return to the example of segmentation to support new-car marketing campaigns, an *a priori* analysis might yield a segment comprising apparently good prospects for a newly released family vehicle positioned at the top end of the enterprise's offered range. But this analysis might not have taken into account customer attributes concerning sociopolitical or environmental attitudes.

Cluster analysis might, in this example, discover amongst the occupants of the initial segment produced by the *a priori* approach a small (but important) cluster of people who on principal refuse to own or drive a car and instead insist always on using public transport. Or cluster analysis might discover a group of people who refuse to own or drive a car on environmental grounds, and might be susceptible to the idea of buying en electrically powered car (which may or may not represent an opportunity for the business enterprise in question).

Even businesses that achieve the goal of one-to-one marketing will continue to observe and study the formation of affinity groups among their customers. The power of segmentation is such that its use can extend beyond the planning and implementation of marketing campaigns: it can provide a basis for planning and operating the entire business.

A critical corollary to the need for segmentation analysis of customer data is the need for sufficient qualities of sufficiently rich customer data. The more primitive, surveillance-based marketing initiatives traditionally used data sourced from operational systems, which was usually fragmented, inconsistent in terms of structure and content, partially incomplete, of variable quality and sometimes inaccessible. These disadvantages have been partially overcome by data warehousing, and so segmentation at least then had available data that was more integrated, cleaner, more consistent, and more accurate. But this data was still essentially based on transaction data, and therefore still resulted in a surveillance style of marketing. But there is a more fundamental inadequacy of the data traditionally used in marketing segmentation efforts, whether that data was taken directly from transaction systems themselves or from data warehouses that have derived their data from transaction systems. Such data is rarely sufficiently rich in terms of the scope and number of customer attributes it encompasses.

This situation has created a mutual dependency between customer segmentation and customer dialogue. Dialogue with customers is clearly an essential element of customized marketing for individual customers, but dialogue cannot bring substantial benefits to the customer or the enterprise unless it is intelligent, which means it has to be based on structured analysis of customer attributes and behaviour. Segmentation provides the means for achieving such analysis, but it requires the availability of detailed, high-quality information about customers. The most effective way to obtain such information is through intelligent dialogue with customers.

Segmentation activities may be categorized according to the customer information used in deciding the allocation of customers to segments. Segmentation categories include:

- Behaviour segmentation, which groups customers according to attitude, usage, or response to a product or promotion.
- Benefits segmentation, which groups customers according to the different kinds of benefit they seek from the product.
- Buyer-readiness segmentation, which groups customers according to the different stages that consumers normally pass through during the purchase process. These usually comprise awareness, knowledge, preference and conviction.
- Demographic segmentation, which groups customers according to demographic variables such as age, gender, family size, income, occupation, education, language, religion, race and nationality.
- Ethnic segmentation, which groups customers according to the needs and strengths of ethnic communities or on the basis that they share a common, recognized heritage.
- Geographic segmentation, which groups customers according to geographic factors such as country, region, climate and population density.
- Interaction segmentation, which groups customers according to their preferences regarding channels, payment methods, promotions and communications.
- Lifecycle segmentation, which groups customers according to their changing needs at different stages of their lives.
- Loyalty segmentation, which groups customers according to different degrees of loyalty to supplier or brand.

- Occasion segmentation, which groups customers according to their consumption of a product or service in certain situations, in response to particular events, or at particular seasonal or cyclical times.
- Profitability segmentation, which groups customers according to the degree of customer value to the enterprise (usually measured in terms of profitability).
- Psychographic segmentation, which groups customers according to different degrees of lifestyle, social behaviour and personality characteristics.
- Usage segmentation, which groups customers according to different degrees of their level and type of usage of product or service.

The only one of these segmentation models that takes the perspective of the consumer is benefits segmentation. This model poses the important question, 'what is it that the consumer is actually buying?'. Despite the impression given by many marketing campaigns customers do not buy product features (those physical or practical aspects of a product that facilitate its function) but actually purchase benefits (those solutions or satisfactions that the customer derives from using the product). From a consumer viewpoint there is a wide range of different motivations, that include the following:

- Initial economic value proposition (what does it cost to buy?)
- Ongoing economic value proposition (what does it cost to run?)
- Personal values value proposition (what are the ethics of the supplier?)
- Stability value proposition (will the supplier be around as long as I will?)

- Aesthetic value proposition (does it look good?)
- Convenience value proposition (does it save me time?)
- Usability value proposition (is it easy to use?)
- Reliability value proposition (does it go wrong?)
- Availability value proposition (is there always someone there?)
- Product value proposition (does it do exactly what I want?)
- Courtesy value proposition (do they respect me?)
- Brand value proposition (does it improve my image?)
- Service-level proposition (if something does go wrong, will they fix it quickly?)

Technical Analysis of Segments

Four separate techniques are used to evaluate the quality and reliability of segmentation models. These are the study of confidence, bias, separation and lift.

Confidence is the extent to which the dialogue questions to which the customer did not respond can affect the degree of assurance of that customer's scores and placement in segments. A low confidence rating indicates that the segmentation process has determined a result but there is uncertainty about how accurately the customer has been placed in segments. This is used only with the scored and scalar segment population mechanisms. Confidence is the degree to which the responses that the customer *did not* supply affect the degree of assurance of their scores and their placement in segments. A low confidence rating implies that the segmentation has determined a result but is not sure of the accuracy. The confidence is based on the number of questions actually answered, compared to the total number of questions asked. This value is further modified for the importance of the missed questions.

Bias is the degree to which the questions, answers and association rules are loaded towards placing a customer in one segment over another, assuming an average response from customers. Bias can be unconscious (which may be corrected) or conscious (which may be intentional but should be noted). The existence of bias in a model may or may not be significant in terms of the expected results. There are too many factors involved in the process of understanding bias to allow a complete automation of bias analysis. Principal amongst these is knowledge of the characteristics of the responding *and* non-responding populations. For example, assume that two segments to be identified are Insomniacs and Normal Sleepers, and that the placement of a respondent will be through several weighted questions rather than outrightly asking the obvious question. If 10% of the human population are known to be insomniacs, whilst 90% are not, then a weighting that results in 90% of respondents entering the Normal Sleeper segment looks correct, even though this may be achieved through biased answers. So far, the bias is good, rather than bad. However, what if the dialogue is only presented late at night or access to the dialogue is easier at night – it is possible that a higher proportion of the insomniacs will be completing the dialogue compared to the proportion of Normal Sleepers. This knowledge about the people not responding alters the meaning of the bias figures.

Separation is the degree to which a customer's score in the segment to which they have been allocated exceeds their score in other segments. This calculated value is of use only with the scored population mechanism. Separation describes the extent to which a customer's score in their primary segment exceeds their scores in other segments. Primary separation is the difference between the highest and the second highest scores. Secondary separation is the difference between the second and third highest scores. These calculated values are of use only with segmentation models that have been populated using the scored mechanism. Primary separation is the meaningful difference between the highest and the second highest scores, and secondary separation is the meaningful difference between the second and third highest scores.

Lift is probably the most commonly used metric to measure the performance of targeting models in marketing applications. The purpose of a simple targeting model is to identify a subgroup (target) from a larger population. The target members selected are those likely to respond positively to a marketing offer. A model is doing a good job if the response within the target is much better than the average for the population as a whole. Lift is simply the ratio of these values: target response divided by average response.

Conclusions

In the past the value of a customer was relative to the size of the customer. Today, the value of a customer is relative to the importance of the segment to which they belong and the key measures are those of acquisition, retention and penetration. Inevitably, this means that customers who do not belong to any defined segment or cluster (what in clustering jargon are called 'outliers') are actually detrimental to the business. In 1998 the CEO of AT&T could state bluntly that, 'We've gotten a lot smarter about separating the customers we do want from the customers we don't'.[7]

Segments are groups of people who respond similarly and therefore assist in our understanding of how to satisfy and communicate. Segments should not be confused with participative customer forums or serve as a guide to product development. Art appreciation aficionados did not persuade Monet that impressionism would be a good idea or Picasso that there was an appetite for cubism. IBM's main-frame computer customers did not clamour for the invention of the PC. Ted Turner came up with the idea of a 24-hour news channel when there was no documented demand for such a product. No telecommunications industry focus group reported that customers felt a compelling need to use their telephones to take photographs. User groups grind down companies into trivial and industry-specific, and even company-specific enhancements that blindside them to genuine innovation and strategic direction. There is a world of difference between empowering customers to control the interaction with the enterprise and letting customers take over the controls of production. The optimum partnership between producer and consumer is one that places control of innovation in the hands of the producer and control of interaction in the hands of the consumer.

As always when people try to make sense of complex issues, the natural tendency is to break the subject down into smaller pieces. This is done in the belief that each of the smaller pieces will be easier to understand, and that the assemblage of improved knowledge and understanding of all the smaller pieces will result in better-informed decisions across the business enterprise's entire market. One thing not to do when faced with uncertainty and complexity is to increase the complexity by reaching for a strategy of one-to-one. This is an end point arrived at in progressive stages.

There has been a tendency for organizations to oscillate between market segmentation with the goal of increasing market share which relies on a reasonably inexhaustible supply of new prospects, and intensive customer profiling which nudges the organization towards seeking a greater share of wallet. But as has been observed already in Chapter 1 any attempt to mix and match the two approaches is almost certainly doomed to failure because of the bad faith that is created by engaging in a dialogue with customers without being prepared to act on its results.

The information war participants are decisively shifting the perspective from market segmentation to customer segmentation and from a logic of product matching to one of customer matching. There is also a significant shift away from bland demographic measures to more penetrating psychometrics, as well as a definite shift from tangible to more intangible components of the overall customer profile. And there is a move from broad granularity to finer granularity using these intangible measures.

The unreconstructed mass marketing advocates tend to focus exclusively on the process of market segmentation and are concerned only with identifying those consumers who they wish to serve. This is in marked contrast to the new wave of information warriors who are more concerned with identifying what services consumers wish to have. These two approaches are underpinned by polar opposite assumptions concerning customers and are, in fact, fundamentally different methods of segmentation.

Part II

The Decade of Customer Information Exchange

2000–2010

5
The Collapse of Time

From Lapsed to Real

Time as a Product

It is surprising just how much the consumer is aware of the value of their time. One consumer goods company conceded to me that many of their customers, who have difficulty installing the more complex systems that they sell, complain that the cost of installing the system is greater than the cost of purchasing it. This growing frustration with wasting time is exacerbated by the tendency towards performance-based remuneration among, not just the growing numbers of technologically-enabled self-employed, but also among the conventional employee class. People are clearly prepared to pay for time and this has been evident for decades as convenience stores and convenience services have blossomed. Before the advent of the Internet people were conditioned to pay more for convenience. Much of the dot com mania was driven by the fixation that Internet convenience could now be cheaper than conventional retailing and that the bricks and mortar model of retailing would disappear for ever. This proved not to be so.

In many ways the experience we have of e-business suggests to us that many lessons that have been painfully learned by conventional business over decades is now being relearned by e-tailers the world over. Like the surprising discovery that customers are fickle. Or, that the complexities of procurement, cost control, supply chain integration and delivery are not obviated by the creation of a new channel. Or the fact that customers who are bombarded by junk mail tend to form negative impressions of those sending the messages. Or, that customers are initially distrustful of new technology and are reluctant to give money to ephemeral images dancing across their computer screen. But the real problem that has been unmasked in the recent dot com trauma is that all too many of the brand new e-tailers pinned their hopes exclusively on the convenience factor of the Internet without realizing that the entire business model had to be fundamentally different.

As discussed in Chapter 1, all bricks and mortar retailers worship at the altar of the 4 Ps (price, place, promotion and product), which is a proven business model that has worked for them but it is not a business model that will work in cyberspace. The notion of a customer is conspicuous by its absence from the 4 Ps and is central to the workings of e-business. Despite this rather obvious fact many sites created by prominent dot coms seem to have a value proposition that says 'we sell the cheapest branded products in the world and isn't this a convenient way to shop?' This is a value proposition that can be found in the advertising blurb of any discount retailer in a shopping centre near any motorway interchange in the world. E-business vendors who treat their customers as if they were the anonymous consumers browsing through the shelves of a store in a shopping mall are making a big mistake. Customers in cyberspace have declared their identity to suppliers; therefore they expect to have a relationship, and in this expectation they are frequently disappointed.

In the next phase of the Internet boom, we will see the emergence of what is sometimes referred to as the 'Evernet'.[1] The Evernet is a concept that describes an environment where literally billions of high-speed, broadband, multiformat Web appliances are constantly switched on. In such an environment business applications that are not happening in real time will be irrelevant. We are living in blurred time where 'instantaneous communication and computation are shrinking time and focusing us on Speed'.[2]

Psychosocial Impacts of Technology

It would appear that all of our creative and commercial energies are converging on a model of ever increasing stimulation of our senses. The ability of consumers to send and receive messages irrespective of time and place has created a constantly 'switched on' universe of ubiquitous availability. The enablers of ubiquitous availability include the Internet, interactive television and mobile devices and now extend to 24-hour connectivity. We have to ask if mankind has an incipient propensity for constant connectivity and interaction of the kind now being experienced. Do we want to be interrupted as we walk along the street by the store we have just passed telling us 'come back and get the special offer!' To what extent are the extreme levels of churn discussed in Chapter 3 less a product of increased consumer vigilance and more to do with a nervous habit of novelty-seeking? Is habitual restlessness the natural endpoint in this stage of mankind's evolution? What are the implications as the boundary separating work and private life disappear? It would seem as if these social and philosophical issues need to be ventilated more comprehensively before we can know with confidence the emerging shape of the global information age. As mankind becomes more and more centrifugal (tending away from a centre) and less centripetal (tending towards a centre) our capacity for reflection and contemplation diminishes.[3] Real-time culture is also driven by the relentless short-term surveillance of the financial markets that has eliminated any planning activity where the expected benefit does not occur within one or two quarters.

In a world where genuinely value-creating, reflective, 'non-wired' thinking time is muzzled, there is a clear danger of intellectual stasis on a grand scale. This is vividly illustrated in the work environments of large corporations where a vast quantity of information of dubious relevance is circulated to virtually everyone and where technology-induced trivialization has become a marked feature of the work environment. The dissemination of any document of original substance within the enterprise can now be expected to become the focus of hundreds of reactions and commentaries. The introduction of a genuinely innovative point of view on to a message board will enervate the proceedings for weeks on end. In these circumstances more and more people engage in more and more frenetic activity as they attempt to squeeze sustenance from an ever-decreasing volume of genuinely value-adding intellectual activity. The reassurance of constant feedback from wide circulation communities plays to the insecurities of petty supervisors, neurotic peers and mediocre performers. The pathological need to be 'in contact' prohibits the scheduling of any activity that lasts longer than a couple of hours.

Various aspects of electronic and mobile communications have contributed hugely to production efficiencies in industry. For the most part, the usage (and increasing convergence) of mobile telephony, e-mail and e-commerce have made their mark in eliminating unnecessary intermediaries and thereby reducing transaction times and improving the responsiveness of business processes that can now adapt quickly to change. What has gone unnoticed is that the fetish for instant access and response (where the benefits are confined to operational processes that function in present time) is tending to drag all of the corporate participants into the all consuming vortex of mass communication exchange to the definite detriment of any long range planning activities.

The Internet has, in the main, driven this tendency and has perfected the capability to send and receive personalized packets of information to and from consumers. But it would be a mistake to locate the advent of the World Wide Web with this phenomenon, since television has been engaged in short message bursts that we have come to know as 'sound bytes'. As we have become progressively conditioned to constant stimulation we have developed shorter and shorter attention spans.

The mobile telephone has now eliminated the need to be in a particular place to transmit and receive messages. And the advent of the Personal Digital Assistant (PDA) combines in one device the functions of a telephone, personal computer, digital imager, MP3 player, personal organizer, games console, video player and entertainment and news services provider. PDA prototypes are already in circulation that will ultimately replace identity cards and financial services facilities, as all banking transactions can be performed on the device. In addition to sending and receiving messages there is already progress being made in 'positional messaging' technologies where the technology physically locates the user and sends messages from adjacent retailers. The alerts that we configure will be transmitted in real time and the spectrum of messages that we select will be as personalized as the ringing tone. In the end our personality, our wealth, our authority and our values, as well as our memories and data will reside on the PDA. The ability of consumers to send and receive messages irrespective of time and place has created a constantly 'switched on' universe. The Internet will provide a source of endless applications that allow us the freedom to perform any kind of transaction. The key to ubiquitous availability is not the Internet but the mobile devices and the communications networks that sustain them.

History, not to mention everyday experience, teaches us that being in command of more information rarely translates into more leisure time. Availability of more information simply serves to stimulate people more than they were previously stimulated. Share-dealing is an obvious example where, instead of being satisfied with the convenience and cost benefits of online trading, the retail investor has became more and more engrossed in the daily movements of stock that would not have previously occupied their time. Information abundance can contribute to volatility in the enterprise just as it does in the financial markets. In much the same way round the clock global trading allows little time for analysis or reflection before decision makers are compelled to act. The inevitable result of more information is more activity, and the early stage of the information revolution suggests that, if current trends continue unabated, the frenetic levels of individual human activity will ultimately become unsustainable.

The Impact of the Internet on Time

At this point it is useful to review the impact of the Internet generally on the process of marketing. Beyond stating the obvious – that the physical has given way to the virtual – we need to consider how the rules of commerce, and by extension, of marketing, have been changed by this technology. There are, in essence, four fundamental and far-reaching changes that have occurred. These are: the advent of customer detection, location independence, value-proposition transparency and transaction immediacy. The first three of these changes have been addressed elsewhere in this book, but by far the most significant of these changes is transaction immediacy, and it is the least discussed.

One of the most profound impacts of the Internet has been on our perception of time. The elapsed time taken to research, communicate, collaborate, interact and transact has shrunk dramatically. And as our ability to interact speeds up, the planning, product and pricing lifecycles that underpin our commercial environment are collapsing. Routine tasks, like purchasing insurance or a holiday, can now occur in minutes with a degree of research rigour that was simply not possible when the task required days of elapsed time. This relentless compression of lifecycles is fundamentally more important to the future of marketing than the price competition impact of the Internet. We are moving inexorably towards 'real-time'.

It may also be that there is a collapse of 'memory' whereby consumers speed up the process of forgetting. For example, the speed with which private investors have returned to the online brokerage market is indicative of an amnesia that was not exhibited in the aftermath of previous sustained bear markets. It could also be that this 'forgiving' nature of online consumers has more to do with the fact that Internet commerce is more 'self-directed' than 'other-directed'. In other words there is no salesperson harassing the consumer; web pages may be alluring but they are not intimidating. Ultimately it is an information rich environment where the consumer is more inclined to believe he or she is in control. In addition, it is a rapidly changing environment where consumer judgements made by a rational intelligence are not regarded as valid after even a relatively short period of time.

The Internet annihilates distinctions that used to matter a great deal. It blurs the lines between product and service; test marketing and marketing; brand advertising and promotion; content and transaction. As these distinctions shrivel into insignificance, the urgency of the fundamental question intensifies: How should we use these technologies to create and manage relationships with our customers?

In summary, it appears to most Web users that the Internet has failed to live up to its promise and is, in reality, a replacement for catalogue-based mail-order firms. Few mainstream enterprises have figured out a way to make the Web work for them. This situation largely arises from a widespread misconception about the potential of the Web. Instead of being seen as a platform for marketing and order taking the real potential of the Web lies in its potential as a communication device. The current paradigm is one where the user wastes time surfing the Web, perhaps finding something interesting, then struggles to place an order and thereafter receives either no further communication at all or is deluged with unsolicited information. What users want is to log on, register their requirements in a standard format where they exercise control over the information submitted (and what it is subsequently used for) and can return and cancel or amend the registration details as they wish. This presents the opportunity for progress.

Mobile Commerce – Accelerating Time

Like the Internet the mobile world has failed to deliver the bright new dawn promised a decade ago. Exciting possibilities such as location-based positioning (LBP) where the customer's mobile phone could be alerted to opportunities in the immediate vicinity of the device have failed to excite customers. The wireless application protocol (WAP) devices have, like the first fax machines, been a solution in search of a problem. The loyalty packages that were to be designed by mobile telephone operators never amounted to anything more than an undifferentiated refund of call-minutes and have been largely dismantled. The plethora of exciting mobile applications that would herald third generation (3G) Internet-enabled mobile phones have never been unveiled. The proud boast of Deutsche Telekom in the heady days of 3G euphoria that they would become 'Europe's largest bank' has been quietly shelved.

This is not to suggest that none of these predictions will ever come to pass. The fax machine did eventually become ubiquitous due to the irresistible desire to collapse time. But the telephone industry is certainly struggling right now to devise time-sensitive applications that can exploit the real-time potential of their technology.

It is true that the market has been disappointed by the take-up rates for WAP technology. For anyone who has used WAP phones this is easy to understand, since the miniature screen technology is slow and laborious to use. However, the success rate with SPS messaging has been spectacularly successful and has developed a youth cult usage among teenagers in Europe and Japan. The Japanese standard for mobile Internet access has also proved to be more successful than the first stage of WAP and take-up has been more encouraging. The real message is that the principle of mobile messaging has been established. Consumers are very positive about the concept.

The next phase of mobile computing will be the much vaunted third generation (3G) networks which have attracted so much attention because of the astonishing amounts paid for these licences at national auctions across Europe. What 3G promises is bandwidth; the ability to transmit images and to achieve acceptable levels of performance for the average Web surfer. This removes the main obstacle to the growth of mobile commerce since the performance issue effectively goes away. Once this has occurred the applications issue will quickly be resolved since there will be an incentive for application developers to create attractive business and consumer solutions that utilize the 3G technology. The ergonomic issue will never disappear entirely since the screen technology on a small device will remain a limiting factor for the foreseeable future. But the proliferation of palm devices illustrates that the use of such handheld devices is not in itself a major obstacle if the applications and performance that are provided are sufficiently attractive.

The key thing is the nature of the applications. If the applications that are created for m-commerce are the same as those that have been a success for conventional e-commerce they will lose. But if the consumer and business applications are modelled on the strengths of a small constantly available device, then they will succeed. It is features like alerts, updates, reminders and the use of compact multiple choice selection options that will prove successful for the constantly wired consumer. People are not going to surf the mobile Web. Mobile technology is not conducive to passivity. Small handheld devices in the pockets of people on moving trains are not optimized for reaching into the World Wide Web. It will be about the Web reaching out and touching the consumer in ways that the consumer has specified. M-commerce requires its own design and development philosophy and that is now emerging. This might seem like an obvious observation, but much of the grizzled exasperation that one hears when talking about m-commerce is from people who are trying to envisage doing on the mobile what they do at the desktop. This is to miss the point.

It is notable that in Europe, where the WAP technology has had a very rocky start, all the talk was of the 'mobile Internet' whereas, in Japan, where the IMODE standard has been considerably more successful, there was much less focus on the technology, with all the talk instead being about services. SMS was widely utilized in

Japan but did not, initially, enjoy widespread usage in Europe or North America. Now it is widely adopted by adolescents as a chatting forum largely, one assumes, because the nature of their learning environment does not permit ringing telephones or ad hoc breaks for noisy conversations. This 'situational' usage of SMS messaging among European schoolchildren can be contrasted with the 'cultural' origins of SMS adoption in Japan, where it is considered unacceptable to speak on the phone in a public place.

The e-commerce dialogue with the customer is a leisurely affair where the customer is sent a message, reads it when convenient, ponders the implications and, at some point, responds. For some business applications (e.g. I want to shop for an airline ticket for a trip next month) this timeline is absolutely fine. In other situations (e.g. I want to be alerted to any substantive changes in the price of a stock) then we need to have near real-time messages for the customer because the nature of the alert is extremely time-sensitive.

Measuring Message Quality

Many websites incorporate features that require consumers to download additional software to be able to view, while others display their wares to all-comers, but confine sales to one country, state or region. This tendency to broadcast messages only to those cognoscenti who can decode the signal and the opposite tendency to broadcast into deep space requires some considered explanation.

The largest proportion of this investment is directed at what might be termed customer discovery applications. This category, which is focused entirely on building marketing intelligence concerning customers, accounts for 70% of the entire business intelligence investment during the past decade and is not inclusive of applications related to supply chain, fraud detection or risk assessment domains (which also include a considerable degree of customer analysis). So, we are entitled to now enquire into the degree of mass customization that has been achieved as a result of this extensive investment. If we use message quality as a basis for assessment, the answer is not encouraging.

We might start our survey by asking the question, how many customers of a supplier have ever received a customized marketing message? The answer to this question is not negligible. We might then proceed to ask how many customers frequently receive customized messages. The response reduces significantly. Now, if we change to the customer's perspective and pose the question, what proportion of messages are perceived by customers to have been crafted for them personally? In other words, of the total number of messages that the customer receives from a supplier, how many are relevant and timely and triggered by information about the customer that has been analysed by the supplier? The percentage now slips alarmingly. And, finally, to the most relevant question, how many enterprises only transmit customized messages? The positive response rates are now negligible. The reality is that mass customization is not a technique or a process; it is a state of being. The only perspective is the customer's and if the customer receives messages that are generally mass produced with an occasional personalized message interspersed, how can the customer know that the relevance of the message is not accidental? After all, even an organization exclusively dedicated to mass marketing does occasionally reach some consumers with a relevant message; otherwise there would be no point to the exercise. By mixing mass marketing with mass customization the message currency gets debased. By allowing any mass mailings to reach the customer is to ensure that the customer's experience is unchanged from the experience of mass marketing. Where the customer is in receipt of messages not relevant to him or her, (or are not even intended for him or her), the customer has no sense of a personal rapport with the supplier.

If I happen to be walking through Times Square in New York and am approached by a pedestrian seeking directions to the White House and also seeking to interest me in purchasing a top hat, my immediate reaction would be one of puzzlement and perhaps even unease. After all, we are in New York, not in Washington DC and I have given no indication of having a requirement for a top hat. If he continues to enquire into matters that seem disconnected from my sense of reality my confidence in our ability to communicate will diminish. Where dialogue is not rational, or capable of being rendered rational, the natural reaction is to feel unsafe and in a situation where almost anything can happen next. Yet this is precisely the situation engendered by many direct marketing communications that occur between a business and an existing customer. A bad quality message is not neutral. Usually, it communicates that the transmission is in error, which reduces confidence in the competence of the sender. Often it communicates that the sender is irrational, which raises doubts about any relationship that the receiver has with the sender. Occasionally the message screams that the sender is plainly insane!

Consider the discomfort of a non-property owning male health insurance customer receiving invitations from his insurer to consider house protection insurance or the benefits of breast screening. The message tells him that the insurer, in whom he has vested a good deal of trust, has no idea who he is, even though they insisted on some prior date that he disclose a great deal of personal information. Various thoughts may pass through his mind about the validity of the insurance cover that he has paid for or what kind of nightmare might be in store for him if he ever has to process a claim with such people. The negative impacts of personally addressed marketing messages that are irrational are considerably greater than direct marketers will acknowledge. Commentators tend to focus on the irritation impact of junk mail but the negative impacts go deeper. Random direct marketing communications underestimate the human fear of the irrational. Mankind's peculiar horror of the nightmare descent into absurdity is a common feature of human conditioning.

The practice of mass marketing has, to some extent, desensitized consumers to the expectation of quality in marketing communications. The following five categories identify the types of poor-quality marketing messages that we commonly encounter:

- **Untimely message** where the customer is qualified for the message but where the message arrives after the customer has already made a decision.
- **Irrelevant message** where the customer may be, at some stage, qualified for the message but where the message bears no relevance to the needs of the customer now or in the near future.
- **Repeat message** where the customer is invited to submit information that has already been submitted in response to an earlier message or transaction.
- **Unqualified message** where the customer is not qualified for the message, will never be qualified and would be found to be ineligible if he or she did respond.
- **Discordant message** where the customer is qualified for the message and where the message is relevant to the customer at the time it is transmitted, but where the customer frequently receives messages from the same business that are untimely, irrelevant, repeats or unqualified.

If we consider the growing volume of such messages that the average consumer receives annually we can get some idea of the scale of customer cynicism and alienation that exists in the market.

A relevant marketing message has a number of characteristics and a quality message should normally satisfy the following seven rules:

- The message should be relevant to the needs of the customer.
- The message should be relevant to the profile of the customer.
- The message should be consistent with other communications transmitted.
- The message should conform to the permissions registered by the customer.
- The message should be timely in the context of the content of the message.
- The message should be transmitted through the channel most appropriate to the content of the message and the preference of the customer.
- The message should permit the customer to easily respond to the message.

When we wish to make a rough assessment of the sophistication and maturity of a marketing environment, the easiest calculation to make is to measure message quality. Because messages are the visible output of the marketing process they tell us a great deal about the intelligence of the background marketing systems. Observing message quality over time also tells the management of the business how well they are doing in progressing their marketing effectiveness. But there is a catch. In any plan to migrate from primitive message quality to sophisticated message quality there will often be a transitory stage when overall marketing effectiveness may diminish. Businesses alive to the danger will manage and plan for the different stages of a transition in a manner that reduces or eliminates this risk. But the quick fix temptation to launch a few mass communication initiatives will always be present until the new environment has fully taken shape. The temptation to debase the message currency will test the nerve and resolution of those businesses making this journey.

Event Oriented Analysis

This requires a model of life events of a customer and an automated response to these events. For example, there is no reason why a financial firm should not have an automatic response to any change in customer circumstances or lifestyle. An event results from an observation of behaviour by monitoring transactions. It has a strong operational focus and may or may not result in an alert to the customer. By contrast, an alert has a strong analytical focus and usually constitutes a communication to the customer. For example, an online brokerage might have an event trigger that would activate when the level of customer trades went above a certain threshold (i.e. it is something the business is interested in knowing about) and might issue an alert to the customer informing them of a special discount rate (i.e. it is something the customer is interested in knowing about).

In the retail financial company of the future, every major event in the customer's life (salary, marital status, job, address, age) will result in an automated recalibration of the value proposition to that customer. So too will periodic assessments of customer profitability and loyalty. We also use the expression 'event-triggers' in a much simpler context when we talk about events happening in a high-transaction environment like financial services or telecommunications. Examples include when an 'account statement' becomes due, a salary payment isn't received, a loan is paid off, or a pattern of international calls becomes established. Using such events as triggers for communications raises the response rate frequently as much as tenfold to perhaps 30%, 40% or even 50%, with huge savings in mailing costs, and improved customer relationships. Typical alerts set up in a customer intelligence infrastructure may include: sales pipeline and forecast thresholds, customer profitability increases and decreases, customer service load balancing issues, marketing campaign performance issues, customer issue resolution problems, either at an aggregate level or for specific high-value customers, and sales close date discrepancies.

But what sort of events were we using to trigger communications? Well, we would have liked to have used life events (leaving home, getting married, moving home, etc.), but we usually didn't have enough data to categorically identify these events, so usually we used events related to the financial data of the client (loan expiring, change in ratio of spend to income, etc.) and follow up and fulfilment communications to manage the dialogue with the customer. The net effect of these campaigns is to build a much closer relationship with the client because the initial communication is much more relevant to the customer (you could argue that the segmentation and propensity models identify the target audience, and the event identifies when the message is relevant to a member of that target audience), and we further demonstrate our understanding of the relationship with the customer by following up and fulfilling appropriately. The convergence of mobile and Internet has spawned new opportunities to create and deliver new types of services. These include the use of wireless devices to make purchases, to check account balances, to pay bills, to trade stocks and to provide alerts.

The B2C marketplace is shifting towards a more customer- or even buyer-centric environment, where individuals will demand a much higher service component to the products and services they purchase, and shifts in the sales and marketing processes from companies pushing products and services to individuals, to individuals pulling the products and services they need. In that new environment, it becomes difficult to see what producers will specialize in. Perhaps the shift will be away from products and services and towards supporting individuals' life events. Financial services companies could provide moving home support. Insurance companies could provide life emergency support services, and so forth.

Relationship management is predicated on the assumption that the Service Age is giving way to the Customer Age. Suppliers have been used to creating products and services and marketing them to a passive audience. In the Customer Age suppliers will increasingly respond to customer pull. Suppliers will be valued for their capabilities and responsiveness, not their products and marketing, since products will be customized and conventional marketing will be replaced by relationships.

A key assumption of any personalized marketing strategy is that the value of collecting and analysing customer data lies in the discovery of 'events' in the customer's life. These events present both opportunities and threats to the supplier and, by being able to anticipate and respond to these events, suppliers can maximize the value of the relationship. What this requires is that the business learns of events in the customer's life and then for the organization to 'market to that event'. These events are, of course, time sensitive. There is a finite period of time following a significant event when a marketing opportunity exists.

Events are usually arranged in hierarchies whereby high-level event summaries can be analysed (e.g. customer growth indicators), as well as the capability to drill down to lower-level events which identify the specific drivers of business growth. In addition, events tend to be tagged as 'positive' or 'negative' depending on the perceived impact of that event on the business. This has given rise to the popularity of propensity scoring models which assess how likely a certain outcome is to occur in response to a particular event.

It should be noted that many events that occur are highly visible and will come to the attention of key account managers without the aid of information systems. The real value of event-oriented analysis is to discover events (or patterns of events) in a consumer market that would otherwise go unnoticed in the mass of transaction data. Most events that are of interest can be captured from internal data sources within the organization, but some events that have an impact on the fostering of relationships may have to be sourced from external data sources and customer survey data.

There are a wide range of events that are meaningful for marketing purposes. These include service-oriented events such as installations, delays, faults, complaints and satisfaction. Examples of financial events include payments, late payments, disputed payments, change of payment method or payment schedule. Lifecycle events include all of the key lifecycle transitions such as marriage, job promotion, moving home, arrival of children, asset purchase and retirement. Sales events will normally be those events that signal purchases made by the customer as well as the responsiveness of a customer to a campaign or promotion.

The pioneers of event analysis have tended to be the financial services industry where, typically, there are over 50 events identified which offer a clear marketing opportunity. This number is likely to be exceeded by the retail sector where product affinity analysis allows for hundreds of events to be discovered. Many events of interest will, naturally, be specific to particular industry sectors or individual companies. Accurate and comprehensive event identification will considerably assist in the task of customizing the service offering and adding value to the relationship with the customer.

Event-oriented marketing techniques are based on the identification of real world customer events and learning how to discover them and market to them. The occurrence of an individual event by an individual customer triggers a marketing message to that individual customer. Event monitoring is a key technique that facilitates the transition from customer segments of many customers to segments of just one customer. For many organizations with disjointed information systems, the events that they desperately need to discover are trapped in the many fragmented operational systems of the enterprise. These event patterns provide the basis for propensity scoring techniques to be used to measure customer loyalty, customer profitability, customer latency, customer responsiveness and help to locate the current status of the customer in the customer relationship lifecycle.

What was the critical factor or range of factors that cause churn? Of course, this question cannot be answered simply since different churn factors apply to different customer segments. The question is complex and the answer can be even more complex. Having responsive systems that allow this issue to be analysed with reference to different data attributes contains the formula for success. The data required to be input in the churn analysis includes demographic data, lifestyle data and behavioural data. Traffic patterns alone or demographics alone or exploring the product mix will not yield a reliable result. All of the data about the customer is required.

It has to be remembered that very many instances of custom disloyalty will not result in any voluntary cancellation event on the part of the customer and can be identified only through an assessment of consumption patterns. Many customers who transfer their business do not terminate their contract, as the extraordinarily large number of dormant bank accounts testifies. It is only from the totality of the data describing the customer profile and behaviour that sound conclusions can be drawn about the extent of customer loyalty.

Conclusions

In the past, communications with customers, including direct mail and outbound telemarketing, were typically outsourced to service bureaus. In addition, it was standard practice for many medium-sized and some large firms to outsource tasks such as deduplication, lifestyle and geodemographic profiling. However, connecting a proprietary database maintained at a service bureau with the real-time customer interaction systems required today is going to prove difficult and costly. It has now become a competitive necessity that every customer touch-point (e.g. Web, telemarketing, customer services and sales) has complete knowledge of the customer. As more integrated technological solutions for real time customer management evolve we will witness the steady insourcing of this key activity.

A true business process starts with the first event that initiates a course of action. It isn't complete until the last aspect of the final outcome is satisfied from the point of view of the stakeholder who initiated the first event. Every marketing initiative gives rise to a marketing process and every process results in an outcome. Traditionally the success of a marketing initiative is measured with reference to the cost of executing the process and the total value of all the positive outcomes. But there is something fundamentally wrong with this calculation; there is a grand assumption that there are never negative outcomes. It is a fallacy that a good quality message is beneficial and that a bad quality message is neutral. A quality message is one where the content and timing of the message is customized for an individual customer who will find the message relevant at the time he or she receives it.

Another common assumption is that the discovery of customer needs provides the first opportunity to market to the customer. But what gives rise to the needs? A key assumption of any customer relationship strategy is that the value of information lies in the discovery of 'events' in the customer's life. These events are time sensitive with regard to exploitation and present both opportunities and threats to the supplier. By being able to anticipate and respond to these events, suppliers can maximize the value of the relationship. In this business model the supplier learns to discover events in the customer's life and then to 'market to that event'.

There is, in the emerging mobile market, a clear contest between the content aggregators and the operators for control of the consumer relationship. Operators have been careful to confine access to their subscribers in order to control the channel to the consumers and this has had the predictable effect of closing many potential distribution channels for mobile content.

In the next phase of commercial innovation the role of technology will not be decisive. Generating more data faster is actually exacerbating the problem. The next stage of development lies not in getting more data, but in learning how to exploit it. In short, we have created an incredible weapon in the armoury of competitive struggle and have only the faintest idea of how we are going to exploit it. As we move from a world of lapsed time business processes to a world of real time business processes we have to recognize the fundamental nature of the transition that has occurred. The real danger lies in continuing to apply the outmoded frameworks that have worked so well for us in the bricks and mortar universe.

Military history records that, at the outbreak of the Second World War, the great powers in Western Europe had a roughly equivalent number of tanks. There were, certainly, variations in terms of the superiority of individual models, the German panzer being superior to other Western models and, in time, inferior to the Russian model. But the key to using these fearsome new weapons of war lay not in the number or, within reasonable limits of variation, on the relative merits of the models. Success lay in knowing what to do with them. In short, success lay in having a strategy to optimize the use of the new innovation. In the eyes of French, British and early Soviet military commanders these weapons seemed most usefully employed as a piece of mobile artillery that was widely distributed to infantry formations where soldiers could cluster behind them as they lumbered forward. But the key to exploiting the new technology lay in forming mass mobile formations of tanks. Blitzkrieg was the 'big idea', not the tank. We can usefully ponder this lesson of history as we consider how to exploit the new technologies of the moment. Grafting new systems on to existing processes is never a recipe for success; the key is to shape new tactics around the new technology. It is true that there are real and substantial changes occurring as we move from physical to virtual, from lapsed time to real time, from message quantity to message quality and from fixed to mobile. But are not the intrinsic characteristics of the new information technologies, such as connectivity, mobility, intelligence or interactivity, such that will revolutionize the lives of consumers; the collapse of time is the big idea. And it is in understanding the implications of that reality that we will discover the applications that will exploit the underlying technologies.

In theory, perfect information produces an environment of perfect prediction. But perfect information in human affairs is never likely to be achieved and it should not be assumed that mere improvements in information lead to greater stability. On the contrary, the dramatic increase in information available to decision makers today has a marked destabilizing effect. Consider the example of the stock markets. The NASDAQ now experiences fluctuations of more than 2% in every two days out of five in contrast to the information-poor environment of 30 years ago when swings of more than 2% were experienced in only one day in every ten. Current financial markets are characterized by a 'dizzying array of derivative products where positions are held for shorter periods in a round-the-clock global trading environment where there is no respite'.[4] What we observe in the financial markets is precisely the same structural transformation that is evident in the information-driven mobile consumer behaviour. Information expands, complexity increases and time collapses. The lesson for all businesses is stark. Build information-based intelligence, absorb complexity and operate in real time.

6
Customer Privacy and Confidentiality

From Surveillance to Permission

The Paradox of Privacy and Personalization

There is an undoubted potential tension between consumer expectations for customized service on the one hand, and consumer expectations for confidentiality and privacy on the other. No marketing initiative, based on improving customer profiles, that fails to address this tension can be expected to succeed. In circumstances where information is used to create a superior value proposition for the consumer, then the interests of the consumer and supplier coincide. But in circumstances where the consumer is subjected to intrusive surveillance for reasons that serve only the interests of the suppliers then the interests of the consumer and supplier collide. We shall never entirely prevent the violation of customer privacy if we are not prepared, to some extent, to limit the surveillance of customer behaviour. And, in limiting the amount of customer observation that is permitted, we also prevent business processes being innovated in ways that are advantageous to the customer. This is the apparent paradox.

When we speak of customer privacy and confidentiality these are actually two separate concerns. Privacy is, by and large, a legal concern that addresses the protection of customer data from abuse by ensuring that the data is secure, accurate, consistent, current and used only for the purpose for which it was collected. Confidentiality of customer data is more difficult to address through the use of legal instruments and is concerned with ensuring that data that is captured by the business is consistent with the requirements of the business process that captures it and that the business exercises prudence in respect of that data. For example, if a customer purchases a motor vehicle why does the vendor wish to know their gender or their age or their level of educational attainment? Provided the customer has a valid driving licence and can pay for the product there is no reason why they should be subjected to prurient enquiries from the supplier. Of course, the marketing department will claim that they need this data in order to construct profiles of the kind of consumer who purchases different kinds of car, but it is less clear what the value is to the consumer who is submitting the information. The general principle is that the provision of such data is discretionary and the consumer should be clearly advised that it is discretionary. But this rarely happens. But more important is that data of which the customer is not even aware is being captured and the business transaction in which the customer is engaged is in no way dependent on them knowing. The most insidious surveillance that occurs is through the use of 'cookies' that track every click stroke made on a website. A cookie is a unique identifier that a web server places on a consumer's computer and can survive after a user has upgraded their browser or changed their Internet service provider.

But there are limits to customer knowledge. No matter how intimate the relationship is between supplier and customer there will always be a level of deliberate concealment by both parties. Few customers are prepared to trade all of their information to all-comers and many customers will choose to trade parsimoniously and infrequently.

Likewise there are few suppliers who will guarantee terms and conditions into the future or make binding commitments in a global environment that is subject to continual shocks and dislocations. This too is a paradox inherent in the concept of relationship marketing. Particularly on the part of the business seeking (or seizing) the information, there is a distinct lack of willingness to enter into any binding or specific commitments with the customer in exchange for the information.

It is undeniably true that microsegmentation will reinforce customer identity. This will not always be good for customers since it will reinforce negative as well as positive self-image. In the mass markets that preceded information-based business practices, negative customer profiles are hidden just as surely as positive profiles are also lost in the homogenous blend. If everyone is to get their 'just desserts' is it a zero sum game where there have to be winners and losers? And what are the sociopolitical implications of such a development? The dangers are that corporate control of knowledge, information, entertainment and technology will provide a tremendous concentration of corporate power without any countervailing restraints. In a *Business Week* cover story in 2001 the question is posed whether it is unfair to treat different customers differently and customer differentiation is described as 'the new consumer apartheid'.[1] Ultimately, is this empowering or disempowering for consumers in general?

One positive feature of the information wars, from a consumer perspective, is that free market economies that are designed to prevent a dominant monopoly and also serve to forestall any large scale concentration of customer information. In *The Lexus and the Olive Tree* Thomas Friedman observes that 'Rule #1 of the Internet Age is that we are all connected but nobody is quite in charge. That is, the Internet is Orwellian in its reach, but there is no Big Brother.

What there is instead of Big Brother is a lot of Little Brothers'.[2] This fact reinforces the authority of the consumer since consumers can, and do, frequently change their allegiance from one business provider to another. It is only in circumstances where the customer is compelled to disclose information to a single source or where an effective information cartel operates (whereby information is shared by competitors) that the spectre of totalitarianism appears.

Involuntary information disclosure is an increasingly sinister aspect of the information age. There is an understandable disquiet as a world emerges where 'agents' controlling domestic devices or even our financial transactions behave like independent decision makers in their own right. The fears arising from ubiquitous chipping of objects and individuals has led one privacy advocate to declare that 'if consumers fail to oppose these practices now, our long-term prospects look like something from a dystopian science-fiction novel'.[3]

It may seem odd that a consumer reacts with delight when the friendly barman of their local bar or friendly innkeeper at their week-end hideaway greets them warmly and never fails to remember their special requirements, but immediately feels threatened when a corporation demonstrates that it has retained a 'memory' of their requirements. On the other hand, accessing e-mail content seems reasonable to many people, including legislators, who would be aghast at the prospect of the Post Office steaming open their mail and keeping a copy of the contents. It will be interesting to see how legislature will handle these distinctions.

Privacy statements are used as a means of reassuring consumers, but these are usually confined to telling us what a business will not do with the data rather than telling us what it is they are doing with the data or, more importantly, why it is that they need the data.

It seems to be an iron law of human nature that it is less onerous to commit ourselves to not doing something rather than to commit ourselves to doing something. As a result of this general tendency, privacy statements are often an evasion of responsibility rather than an expression of a genuine compact with the consumer. In any event, the vast majority of privacy statements that are published amount to no more than an undertaking not to do anything illegal with the data which is an assurance that ought to be superfluous in any contractual relationship.

There are two schools of thought concerning the privacy issue, in general, that are frequently aired. One school of thought suggests that we have reached the high point of customer data exploitation and that the opportunity to share data between companies or even to use customer data to cross-sell products within companies will be more and more curtailed as regulations are tightened in the name of customer confidentiality. The alternative viewpoint is that the current interest in privacy issues has been brought about largely by the adverse reaction of a frustrated public to the junk mail that is the temporary phenomenon of the early and crude efforts to exploit data. In this scenario, as we become more sophisticated in targeting customers, the concept of mass circulation junk mail will recede and consumers will react more positively to targeted campaigns that introduce consumers to buying opportunities in which they are genuinely interested or from which they can benefit as individuals. Whichever scenario comes to pass consumer privacy and Internet security issues have been appearing for the past five years as the top issue in information-based commerce.[4]

The test of whether a relationship exists with someone is determined by whether there is some level of intimacy with that person. The absence of intimacy betrays the non-existence of a relationship.

Obviously, if we transmit the same message to 50,000 customers or one million customers then we can hardly make claims on intimacy. But where an established and trusted dialogue is established there is no guarantee of full disclosure. In efficient trading conditions the customer would constantly be presented with engaging value propositions and would choose to trade or transfer their information on the basis of value and utility. In a free market for customer information the goal of coaxing the consumer to part with information would be an intrinsic part of all of the customer interface processes.

Classes of Consumer Information

Not all data that is stored about individuals is data that has been submitted by individuals or even data that the individual is aware exists. When we speak of consumer data and its protection and disclosure there are four classes of data about individuals that can be considered. These are perfect data, imperfect data, passive data and derived data.[5]

- **Perfect data** is data that is known to refer to an individual and is specifically associated with an individual's name, address and date of birth. It includes all data that that individual has disclosed through the use of forms, surveys, transactions or specific marketing solicitations.
- **Imperfect data** is data that is likely to refer to an individual but is associated with an account such as a credit card, or a device such as a telephone or Internet browser (which may have more than one user or may be used by an individual on behalf of other individuals).
- **Passive data** is data that is not submitted by an individual but is captured through a process of observation such as click-stream

data, usage history or any other data that is generated through a process of monitoring the behaviour of the customer.

- **Derived data** is data about an individual that is inferred from other data that is available and is derived from combining two or more attributes of data that are known about the individual and by using assumptions based on the mathematical models that are used to create profiles.

The consumer is always aware of what personal data, whether perfect or imperfect, they have supplied to a business. But the consumer is not generally aware of what passive data they are continually supplying, based on intrusive surveillance, or through profiles that may be derived about them based on assumptions that may or may not be correct assumptions. It is these last two classes of data that are the most contentious in the context of customer privacy.

Sociopolitical Impact of Information

If land, labour, capital and machines defined the basis of wealth in the old economy, then intellectual property provides the basis for wealth in the knowledge economy. And a very significant portion of the intellectual property that is essential to success in the new economy will be knowledge of individuals. Therefore, it is inevitable that strenuous efforts will be made to ensure that our personality, wealth, authority, values, associations and history will be captured and analysed. In other words, individual identity may well become a commodity to be traded in the market, which raises a host of ethical issues.

The topic of computer ethics first surfaced in the 1980s when it was perceived that technological changes had outpaced ethical developments, bringing about unanticipated problems that have caused a 'policy vacuum'. What emerged at that time was the PAPA group that defined privacy, accuracy, intellectual property and access as the four critical issues to be addressed.[6] The privacy question was defined in terms of what information an individual was obliged to disclose and what information an individual had a right to keep to themselves. Accuracy relates to the fidelity of the information that is disclosed and the rights of redress of an injured party where the information is not correct. Property addressed the key question of ownership of personal information and the allocation of a value to information property that is traded. Accessibility addressed the threat of exclusion that hangs over those who are not technologically literate or who are otherwise excluded from access to the benefits of an information society.

An individual's claim to privacy is justified on the basis of the logic of ownership (i.e. an individual possesses his or her own information and has a right to exercise full control over it). This right includes the discretion to disclose, conceal, sell, exchange or alter that information. Therefore, the main ethical question is centred on the issue of theft of information that is the sole property of the individual being described. For example, a number of individuals in different jurisdictions have sought to patent their own genetic information on the grounds that this belongs to them as individuals and that pharmaceutical companies have no entitlement to gain sole and proprietary ownership of this information. The same logic applies to personal information stored by commercial organisations about consumers.

Because of the remoteness of the process of surfing in cyberspace and the virtual interaction that occurs with faceless individuals, there is a danger that all people to some extent, and some people to a considerable extent, will perceive it to be 'unreal'. In this dreamlike state their actions may seem as insignificant as playing an arcade game. The virtual and anonymous nature of the environment as well as the corresponding depersonalization of interaction that can occur can have unfortunate consequences. These include a diffusion of responsibility, a diminished ethical sense and a perceived lack of accountability. The fact that the individual is aware (whether consciously or vaguely) that they are disclosing their own essence as well as being cleverly manipulated adds to the sense that they are in an ethically neutered environment. This is accentuated by their awareness that most of the SPAM messages they receive are traceless and placeless. Even in circumstances where the novelty of the virtual experience has worn off and a more real sense of engagement is experienced by users there remains a sense that individual uniqueness is undermined by the process of profiling. But even the most militant advocates of privacy must acknowledge that the disclosure of some information about ourselves is a price we must pay to be recognized as members of society and to be able to function effectively in it.

A concrete example of the danger of impulsive behaviour, where the user may feel disconnected from reality is in the area of online investing. In the year 2000 the SEC felt it necessary to issue a stiff warning to users of the new medium regarding the dangers of undisciplined online investing. By 2002 more than 37% of all retail stockbroking orders in the US were entered via the Internet and by the end of 2003 the number of online brokerage accounts exceeded 35 million.[7] The benefits include lower transaction costs and ease of access but the downside includes the risks of impulsive and ill-considered investment decisions. Ease of access cuts both ways.

Another threat presented by information is the steady erosion of social solidarity in matters such as insurance. In the world of information scarcity customers purchased insurance because the incidence of illness or disaster was regarded as a random event which might strike anyone down with equal unpredictability. But in a world where information regarding medical disorders or a genetic propensity to a particular illness is becoming more available, the concept of sharing community risk may be obsolete. It seems to be the case that insurance companies are using such information to better manage actuarial risk, but the extensive use of such information by insurers may be short sighted. Insurance works on the basis of fortuity. A world where we are able to predict the lifespan of individuals or provide long-range weather forecasts is a world where the concept of insurance is redundant.

Fears are also expressed that, just as individual relationships between business and consumers sounds the death knell of the mass market, so individualized interactions between the state and citizens are corrosive of the concept of society. But it is not at all clear whether political processes will necessarily emulate commercial ones. One obvious reason is that the apparatus of government is necessarily monolithic and individual citizens cannot cherry pick different services from different countries where they do not hold citizenship. Therefore, while there will be a tendency towards individualization of consumption-related services provided by the state, mass mobilization of political groupings is likely to remain a permanent feature of political life in democracies. Indeed, there are good reasons for believing that technology will facilitate the mass mobilization of citizens.

Therefore, the outstanding ethical problem can be separated into four distinct issues. The first and most fundamental, is the improper acquisition and use of someone else's property. The second is the instrumental treatment of a human being who is reduced to a mere packet of information. The third is the danger presented to individuals to act rashly or impetuously. The fourth is discrimination that may be applied to an individual, whether accidentally or intentionally, based on the profile that is created.

Providing Legislative Remedies

One obvious remedy to the ethical dilemmas posed is through legislation. But there has been a marked reluctance by legislators to address the issue comprehensively or to even define in concrete legal terms the rights and obligations that apply in this area. For example, does privacy simply mean the right to ensure that data is not shared or transferred to third parties? Or does it mean that consumers can decline altogether to provide information? Does it mean the ability to review the data that is collected and does it include authority to challenge, modify, disable, or delete information? This last question was posed in the introduction to the final report of the advisory committee of the US Fair Trade Commission on Online Security and Access in May 2000. The answer was inconclusive with the committee failing to agree on a single appropriate type of access for every situation and instead outlined a range of options.

Reluctance to legislate is also based on the practical problem of how to ensure compliance when websites can be located outside of the jurisdiction of the nation state. There is also the fear that rigorous compliance within the boundaries of a jurisdiction would have the effect of denying businesses in that jurisdiction the ability to effectively participate in the largest growth industry in the world. This reality has not stopped the European Union from prohibiting the hosting of consumer data about European citizens outside of Europe. Nor was the insidious nature of the Internet envisaged when the US Supreme Court ruled in 1970 that 'Congress has erected a wall, or more accurately, permits a citizen to erect a wall that no advertiser may penetrate without his acquiescence'.[8] How these provisions may be enforced is unclear in an environment where consumers are enthusiastically engaging with the global Internet and where so much of the SPAM originates in jurisdictions which have no legislation whatsoever governing such activities. Europe reserves the right to place a 'data embargo' on countries that, in the opinion of the European Union, do not have an adequate data protection regime. This has led some libertarian commentators in the United States to speculate about the potential for a trade war over the issue.[9] The stakes are certainly high and the potential for conflict is real.

In addition to the practical obstacle of enforcement, there is the very real fear that most legislators have only a very superficial grasp of the issues involved and their endeavours might result in distorted and unintended consequences. There is also a general acknowledgement that technology will change faster than the law. This leads some legislators to urge caution until the shape of the information environment crystallizes, while others urge action now before they lose the opportunity to influence the outcome.

Legislators have also been influenced by the positive global political influence of the unregulated Internet in providing access to information in many totalitarian societies and have perceived the Internet as a positive agent in the dissemination of liberal democratic ideas. As the influential philosopher Francis Fukuyama observed at the beginning of the 1990s, 'A true global culture has emerged, centring on technologically driven economic growth and the capitalist social relations necessary to produce and sustain it'.[10] Acceptance of this rationale has contributed to the reluctance by politicians in the Western liberal democracies to place barriers, at this stage, on the growth of the Internet. But, in recent times, the debate has shifted and reflects a growing realization that an unregulated Internet may be corrosive of individual freedom as well as reinforcing of it.

The scarcity of information, where the scarcity is equally experienced by all competitors in a market, has the effect of harmonizing the business model. Where the outcomes of various options are not known with any confidence there is a tendency to be averse to change because it is truly the unknown. And where the value proposition from each supplier is roughly equivalent, then the focus for differentiation tends to focus exclusively on the efficient exploitation of capital. By contrast, in an environment where information is plentiful, the pursuit of change is rendered safer. In such circumstances, the focus of business strategy shifts to growth. This conclusion presents an interesting dilemma since it can be argued with equal cogency that the information-intensive competition will serve to accelerate global consolidation or, alternatively, will facilitate large numbers of new entrants. Which scenario will come to pass will largely be determined by whether information about the market is controlled by suppliers or by consumers. This is the essential political question to be addressed.

Public interest in the issue of privacy has been sporadic and has arisen usually in response to specific instances of abuse. For example, the sale of the electoral register in the UK to businesses for marketing purposes has caused some controversy there. In 1998 a British cabinet minister observed that 'the practice (of providing copies of the electoral register to commercial organizations) is controversial and unpopular with many members of the public, so much so that some people may even be reluctant to register to vote'.[11] While this comment invited the obvious response that it is more dangerous to a democracy to have a secret register of electors or one that cannot be copied and scrutinized, it does provide an example of the simmering discontent that was beginning to surface in many countries. A few months before this controversy erupted in the United Kingdom the FCC in the United States tightened regulations among telephone operators regarding the use of data collected about customer usage patterns. The FCC regulation banned the use of customer data collected by telecommunications operators for a purpose other than the purpose for which it was being used by the operators (ordered in February 1998). However, it is clear that legislators find it difficult to define the provisions of such protection clearly. How does one define what an electoral register may be used or not used for and how does one precisely define the purpose for which a telephone company collects information? It was clear that matters will not rest there.

The one area that legislators in Europe and the US have addressed is the problem of SPAM. These unsolicited contacts and communications are egregiously invasive in the lives of citizens and have, in particular, exposed e-mail users to a gigantic volume of irrelevant, often offensive and time wasting communications. SPAM is generally seen as a nuisance to individuals, but within large organizations it is much more of a serious issue. According to the European Commission SPAM cost European businesses nearly $3bn in lost productivity in 2003 alone. In addition there are the regulatory requirements imposed on many industry sectors, most notably the financial sector, requiring them to maintain all communications for a number of years. Increasingly the greater portion of data being expensively maintained by these institutions is not genuine consumer communications but the growing mountain of junk that is received daily.

In the US the 2003 legislation on SPAM states that, 'It is unlawful for any person to initiate the transmission of any commercial electronic mail message unless the message provides – (ii) clear notice of the opportunity to decline to receive further messages from the sender'.[12] This is, in effect, a provision that allows citizens the right to decline to receive any further communications from the sender but does permit the initial communication to be transmitted. In effect, it places the onus of responsibility on the recipient. By contrast, the European Union legislation introduced in the same year places the onus of responsibility on the sender. European legislation states, 'A person shall not use or cause to be used any publicly available electronic communication service to send an unsolicited communication for the purpose of direct marketing by means of electronic mail, or by automated calling machine or facsimile machine, to a subscriber, who is a natural person, unless the person has been notified by that subscriber that for the time being he or she consents to the receipt of such communication'.[13]

Most countries have legislative provision to allow citizens to access, examine and, in some circumstances, amend information that government holds about the individual citizen. But this transparency does not extend to commercial organizations. This distinction was drawn by Senator John McCain in an exchange in the US Senate in 2001 when he questioned why, if he was entitled to gain access to personal information held by government agencies under the Freedom of Information Act, had he not the same right to access information and personal profiles held by commercial companies.[14] Ironically, the reason most companies give for failing to make personal information available to customers is that they have not figured out yet how to integrate it into one place.

Up until this point it seems to be the case that the drive for greater consumer protection has been at the initiative of legislators and activist groups rather than the general public. Public concern has largely been confined to expressing irritation that arises from very dumb marketing techniques rather than concern at the pervasiveness of intelligent marketing techniques. As the scale and implications of intensive behaviour surveillance becomes evident to the public we can anticipate that concerns about privacy will steadily intensify and, in time, will become a mainstream political platform. Therefore, it is likely that we have not seen the end of legislative efforts to grapple with the problem.

But it is notable that, in the measures taken so far, two distinct approaches to the question of protecting the privacy of customer data have been adopted by the European Union and the United States respectively. In the European Union the approach has been to enforce a regime where the consumer has to 'opt-in' to a marketing programme, while the legislative philosophy in the United States has been to safeguard the ability of consumers to 'opt-out'. This is where matters now stand.

Confusion about the civil liberties implications of the Internet in particular, and the holding of personal information in general, has yet to be resolved. Early US concentration on keeping the Internet free of government regulation seemed to be an instinctive manifestation of a First Amendment Rights regard for individual freedom. European endeavours to address the issue were also rooted in fidelity to preexisting principles such as the European Convention for the Protection of Human Rights and Fundamental Freedoms which states that 'everyone has the right to respect for his private and family life, his home and his correspondence'. Proceeding, as they did, from different starting points, it is perhaps unsurprising that they have both ended up in different places.

The Concept of Permission

'Here's information about my product, whether you want it or not' is the all-familiar refrain of indiscriminate interruption marketing.

This approach has been challenged recently by the concept of 'permission marketing'. Permission marketing provides the consumer with an opportunity to volunteer to be marketed to, and by volunteering; the business has a greater degree of confidence that the consumer will pay attention to the marketing message. The marketing message becomes one that is anticipated, personal and relevant.[15] Permission marketing does not barge in assuming that a prospect wants the product/service on offer, but instead seeks the non-transferable permission of the consumer before transmitting a marketing message. In a world where the attention of consumers is finite, and where mass marketing techniques seek constantly to dominate the amount of attention that is available, permission marketing offers the consumer a way of controlling who it is that enjoys their attention. The basis of permission marketing is that the prospective customer is provided with an incentive to volunteer to be subjected to a marketing campaign. Bill Gates has observed that 'if salespeople want to contact you and you've set a price for the privilege, they can decide whether it's worth the potential cost'.[16] The benefit to suppliers of permission marketing lies in the fact that the prospects are actively interested in listening to the marketing message. The waste of resources and the customer irritation associated with mass marketing are therefore eliminated. The theory of permission marketing is that the customer is engaged in the marketing process and will consent to receiving communications on specific subjects where they have registered an interest. Undoubtedly, this state of affairs is a happy antidote to the horrors of endless junk mail, but is it what customers really want?

The take-up of permission marketing since it was first proposed has been disappointing and many suppliers have been reluctant to engage with the idea. Many businesses where the marketing philosophy is firmly rooted in the manipulation and exploitation of customers are, unsurprisingly, resolutely opposed to the concept of permission. But many other businesses broadly sympathetic to the concept have been timorous in their adaptation of the idea. The reasons provided for this lack of nerve are numerous and include the fact that customers have first to be interrupted in order to gain their permission (not an encouraging start) to the fear that, by asking permission, you run the risk of being refused and that might lead to the cessation of all communications. But the most frequent objection is based on the fact that most businesses have an enormous sunk investment in surveillance-based systems where they hope to be able to gain intimate insight into customer requirements without gaining their permission. In effect, they do not need, they believe, the cooperation of the customer in order to discover how to craft meaningful and personalized offers.

Most customers want to receive information about products or services that they are intending to purchase and they want to receive this information within a restricted time window prior to the purchase decision. Ideally, they do not want to have to engage in extensive research in order to make the purchase decision and would welcome any additional information that would assist them. And they, most resolutely, do not want to be subjected to a barrage of information concerning products or services that they are not intending to purchase or have already purchased. The principle of permission marketing is to facilitate the customer to 'register' to receive information about specific products within a specific period of time. But register 'where'? Customers, it is argued, may not have the time or inclination to register their requirements in many different places.

To work most effectively permission marketing is more likely to be a brokered service where a brokerage agency would communicate a customer's permission to a complete range of vendors who supply that product or service. The most promising segment of the market to act as brokers is the Internet portal sites (such as AOL, Yahoo!, etc.) which already have large subscriber databases. In the bricks and mortar world many customers already have customer relationships with brokerages who may seek permission to market a range of financial products from different financial institutions. Inevitably, customers will, over time, develop an expectation that the broker will provide more than mere access and will add value to their service offering evaluations and recommendations. This would signal a complete transformation of the business model and would negate any benefits that might accrue to those suppliers who would use the permission lists, unless they happened to be recommended by the list broker. It remains to be seen whether the keepers of the permission lists could resist this obvious consumer demand while maintaining the loyalty of their business subscribers.

The use of permission lists by some individual firms, where existing customers or known prospects agree to receive specific promotional material is occurring. This is an advance on mass mailing but is also an acknowledgement by the supplier organization that they do not know nor understand the customer's needs. From a consumer perspective the use of permission marketing by their suppliers runs the risk of alienating customers who expect the supplier to know what they want when they want it without having to be told. For example, if I have purchased wine from the same wine region, similar price range and similar vintage from an online wine seller for a number of years and I get an enquiry from them asking me what kind of wine I like to buy, my reaction may be one of stupefaction. In addition, the act of conferring on customers the authority to determine what, if any, communications they wish to receive runs the risk that very many customers will not agree to receive any promotional material at all.

The concept of permission marketing, as it is practised, usually involves some form of incentive to encourage prospects to volunteer to be subjected to a marketing campaign. Over time the incentives will need to be refined and expanded in order to ensure that the permission is maintained. Incentives may be defined as 'shallow' or 'substantive'. In the world of loyalty cards we have already seen how ineffective are the results of 'shallow' incentives such as the accumulation of points that allow the customer to avail of special offers, discounts or prizes. This kind of incentive locates the supplier organization firmly in the domain of mass marketing and is simply a means of bribing the customer with a view to gaining permission and encouraging loyalty. It is likely that the incentives will have to be constantly renewed and intensified in order to maintain and reinforce the permission. The more effective incentive is to use the information gained through the dialogue with the customer to package service offerings for that specific customer and this approach can be categorized as a stage in achieving a mass customization strategy. It is considerably more difficult to achieve but is also considerably more effective as a marketing strategy.

What we know, to date, about permission marketing suggests that it is still employed as a product-focused strategy that seeks to find more prospects that are interested in purchasing the product or service and the onus is on the customer to declare their needs rather than the enterprise discovering their needs. In this sense the culture of permission marketing seeks to avoid making the necessary investment required to analyse customer behaviour. Instead it is an attempt to continue to pump new prospects into the pipeline in the time-honoured fashion while seeking to mitigate the enormous inefficiencies of the conventional mass marketing approach. Permission marketing seeks to reduce the costs and increase the positive responses of a mass marketing campaign by more selective targeting.

But it remains a refinement rather than a fundamental change in the old and failed techniques.

Sincere, meaningful and personal communication is welcomed by human beings and rarely requires their permission. The goal, therefore, is to blend a strategy of analysis and permissions. Therefore we must inevitably conclude that permission marketing alone, in the absence of customer analysis, is a technique that is designed to prolong and extend the life of a mass marketing culture at a point in history where customers are demanding that businesses remember what they do (i.e. their behaviour) as well as remember what they say (i.e. their permission). This may not have been what the proponents of permission marketing intended, but it does reflect how the concept has been adopted and deployed by many businesses. Seen in this context permission marketing that is exclusively based on 'bait' that lures the customer has all the hallmarks of a transitory stage in the development of the mechanisms for transmitting marketing messages rather than a final destination. The customer does not generally need to be enticed with rewards where they are confident that the service they receive will be transformed in their favour if they participate in the exchange contract. The ultimate goal of marketing strategy still remains the eclipsing of all mass marketing techniques with one-to-one communications based on a thorough knowledge of customer requirements, a sophisticated customer lifecycle map, a high degree of responsiveness to customer events and a high degree of trust being engendered in the relationship.

The Impact of the Internet on Privacy

The greatness of the Internet is that it is a global collective, and this fact is peculiarly calculated to make it intolerant of regulatory incursions by governments. Now, in addition to this fact, which is general, there are those specific failures to control information on the Internet that have been experienced by 'portals', the gates to the kingdom that the user has selected to pass through regularly. Thus far, the full extent of the e-commerce information strategy has been to try to secure these gateways and entice the consumer onto an attractive hassle-free and monopolistic transit system. Why? Because you can then find out where they are going, how long they stay and what interests them. But there is no guarantee that, once they are safely delivered into the kingdom, they will not wander off the radar screen of the portal owner and wander freely and anonymously where they please, or more likely, hop onto the radar of some other portal. This has been the actual experience. All of which suggests that the Internet may be beyond the control of either governments or commercial organizations.

The difference that electronic commerce makes is to elevate information to a higher value. Information is a prerequisite for inhabiting an electronic commerce world. It is no longer a separate asset to be reviewed periodically. It is not even any longer fuel for turbo-charging the operations of the business. It now becomes intellectual capital without which a business cannot be established. Control of information, not passage, is seen to be the differentiator in the information wars. So we are looking, not at a conventional struggle for market share in this new marketplace, but a scramble for information capital.

The technological development of the information economy is happening at an alarming pace and each influence has been barely analysed before the next wave of innovation sweeps us on. But the tides of innovation have, for the most part, been physical as we learn to capture exchange and store different individual atoms of information in ever expanding databases. We have not been able to keep intellectually abreast of the potentialities to exploit information but, more importantly, we are also struggling to redefine the new relationship that needs to exist between business and consumer.

The Case for Self-Regulation

There has been concerted lobbying from technology and business industry sources to prevent government from placing constraints on the acquisition and use of consumer data. Many firms engaged in electronic commerce, or in the provision of hardware or software technology to enable electronic commerce, reinforce this point by including references to it in their safe harbour statements filed with regulatory agencies. The following is a typical sample of such a statement: 'If new laws or regulations prohibit us from using information in the ways that we currently do, or if users opt out of making their personal preferences and information available to us and our affiliates, the utility of our products will decrease, which could have a material adverse effect on our business, operating results and financial condition. If personal information is misused by us, our customers or our network affiliates, our legal liability may be increased and our growth may be limited'.[17] In circumstances where such statements declare to investors that there is a risk that government intervention will adversely affect profits it is clear that government will act cautiously for fear of killing the technology 'golden goose' that has driven the growth of the global economy to such dizzying heights.

The broad thrust of the platform against legislative remedies is that burdensome regulations place at risk an industry that has created millions of jobs, is fuelling the growth of the economy, bringing the world closer together and which will, given time, introduce a regime of self regulation that will be driven by the market pressure of consumer demand. Because the Internet is a new frontier, an open marketplace with few barriers to entry, premature and ill-conceived legislation would have the effect of retarding the growth of electronic commerce. The argument also draws attention to the costs and complexities that would be imposed by regulation as well as the benefits to the consumer of personalization.[18]

The argument is also put forward by industry sources that full disclosure of customer profiles would have the effect of revealing to competitors the techniques used by firms to classify customers by unmasking the data mining algorithms and underlying assumptions of their profiling models. This, the industry say, would be a breach of their intellectual property rights. Precisely how one can justify a tenacious defence of corporate intellectual property rights while at the same time dismissing the information property rights of individuals is simply another contradiction that remains unresolved.

Business organizations that have invested heavily in acquiring customer information will naturally see it as a valuable asset and the desire for self regulation is motivated by a desire to protect that competitive advantage. In the long run this may become a potentially insuperable barrier to entry into markets where these information barons 'own' the market intelligence. In such circumstances it will be hard going for any new entrant to penetrate a market where they are starting with zero customers and, therefore, have absolutely no knowledge of the customer intelligence landscape. One solution is for all consumers to register their personal and consumer preference data voluntarily on a single, regulated personal, national or global database that is available to all suppliers of goods and services to use for marketing purposes. Needless to say, this idea is even more noxious than government regulation to the established industry players who have invested heavily in acquiring their own proprietary customer intelligence.

Self regulation is achieved by the certification of a business by a third party where the bona fides of the third party are broadly acceptable to the market. This is not new and agencies promoting ethical business practice and consumer rights have been a feature of the market for a long time. But the advent of the Internet has intensified interest in these bodies and has seen new agencies come into existence. In general the requirements of such certifying agencies are broadly similar. Companies wishing to receive the seal of approval must be certified and must allow themselves to be subjected to compliance audits. For website operators wishing to be certified they must agree to disclose all information-collection practices and must permit consumers to refuse the use of their personal data for marketing. In addition they must maintain consumer data in a secure database and they must display their privacy statement prominently on their website. Once certified, the site can display the insignia or logo of the certifying organization so that visitors to the site know the level of privacy and protection that is afforded to them if they do business. The logic is that sites that fail to satisfy the criteria and do not display the logo will be shunned by consumers. The force of the market will compel electronic commerce organizations to take the issue of privacy seriously and this approach will banish the disreputable from the market.

Opponents of self regulation point out that the providers of the seal of integrity are themselves a private concern that charges licence fees for the use of their seal and that removal of the seal from clients will result in lost revenues. The fact that most of these are non-profit organizations does not diminish the suspicion that an over-rigorous stance would impact on the market share and overall survival chances of the certifying organization. It is also observed that such watch-dog bodies cannot replace a regulatory authority that can impose real sanctions and that it is rare for such organizations to report their clients to regulatory agencies for deceptive business practices or breach of legislative provisions concerning privacy. The point is also made that there are multiple organizations in most large countries granting these seals and that this regulatory framework could only function effectively if there were to be two or three well recognized seals globally. But the overriding objection to this form of self-regulation is that it is seen by opponents as an attempt to postpone or substitute legally enforceable privacy rights. The debate between those who favour seals and those who favour statutes will continue.

Conclusions

As we approach maturity in the process of exploiting customer information one of two scenarios will come to pass. Either the information will become the proprietary property of those who have invested in gathering it, in which case the struggle for competitive supremacy will be determined by the goal of achieving monopoly or near monopoly control of consumer information in different markets. From a consumer perspective this is, plainly, a malign scenario. Alternatively, the personal information of individual consumers will remain their personal property to barter for benefits as they see fit, in which case the character of the technological challenge is altered to one of enticing consumers by deploying more attractive applications that generate consumer value. All of the evidence explored in Chapter 3 suggests that the preponderance of combatants in the information wars are focused firmly on the malign scenario but that the preponderance of success that has been experienced thus far has been enjoyed by those who embrace the assumptions of the more benign approach.

However, the ability to exploit customer information for mutual benefit will always depend on having access to it. Therefore, it would be naïve not to entertain the possibility that, over time, the monopolists may have their way.

At present the market environment for information is quite artificial since everything is free and almost anything is possible. It will not remain so for long. The history of change and innovation suggests that each age unfolds in a distinctly nonlinear fashion with checks, shocks and reverses delaying the final outcome. The premise of the inevitability of ubiquitous information is based on the unqualified assumption that anything that can be measured will be measured. We are led to believe that basic human instinct rather than technological capability will ensure this outcome. However, the social and political implications of ubiquitous surveillance of human behaviour have only barely been assessed and it is in this broad political domain that we will encounter the most spirited opposition to information intensive marketing. What can be measured and what will ultimately be permitted, whether by legislation or consumer, is not yet clear. What is clear is that, in the absence of trust, there will be no foundation to create mutual prosperity in the economic spheres produced by new technology.[19]

The critical question that needs to be posed, whether by advocates of government regulation or self regulation or no regulation, is whether a genuine 'exchange' is occurring and who has effective control over it. In a time before the information wars there was a single exchange of information whereby a consumer provided information to a supplier at the commencement of a relationship and, while it would be updated in circumstances where it changed, there would be no further provision of information. Now there is, in theory, a continuous exchange where the consumer is constantly, whether wittingly or unwittingly, supplying information to the supplier and the supplier is continuously adapting and personalizing the service being supplied to the consumer. But is the return part of the exchange actually happening? How many of us supply the continuous information stream and get nothing of any value in exchange? Time is running out for many businesses to demonstrate that they are, in fact, in the exchange business and not just in the acquisition business. In very many cases less high-minded motives than the desire to improve customer service on the part of businesses engaged in gathering information suggest themselves. The extent to which customer information is exclusively used internally by the organization to fine tune business practices and strategies illustrates this point vividly.

For many in the information technology community who are acutely aware of the utterly dysfunctional information environment (explored in Chapter 2) that exists in most businesses today, the idea that the integrity of the customer is under threat any time soon arouses more mirth than concern. But this is not necessarily reassuring since mistaken profiles can be more damaging to consumers than accurate ones, and month by month more battalions are forming up in good order amidst the chaos on the information battlefield. The time is not long off when a critical mass of business participants in the information wars will have achieved personalization effectiveness and, when that happens, those businesses that are still milling around in confusion will be dispatched quickly.

Ultimately, there are two unassailable truths about the practice of marketing in the current century that renders mute much, though not all, of the debate about whether it is governments or businesses that should regulate data protection. The first is that the critical data marketers require is not contractual data, such as disclosure of name, address, gender or date of birth, it is lifestyle and behavioural data.

The second is that customers cannot, under any conceivable circumstances, be compelled to disclose this information. Customers can and do decline loyalty cards, prohibit cookies, skip intrusive questions on forms and pay in cash. In addition, customers unconsciously mask their personal profile by churning their accounts, changing address, changing name, making one-off purchases, making purchases on behalf of other individuals and by changing their minds. Frequently, customers will consciously lay false trails, open multiple online accounts, provide contradictory information and lie. In the final analysis it is the customer who will regulate what lifestyle information they are pleased to provide.

The permission that needs to be sought from consumers is not the permission to be marketed to *per se*, but the permission to be analysed in the context of a real exchange of value. Sooner or later it will occur to most sane businesses that it is considerably cheaper and more effective to establish a compact with customers which will satisfy both parties than to expend large fortunes in the unsuccessful pursuit of making sense of the gigantic volumes of fragmented surveillance data that they are amassing. How this more rational outcome might be achieved is outlined in the following chapter.

7
Closing the Loop

From Monologue to Dialogue

The Concept of Dialogue

Customer dialogue is defined as 'the application of genuine closed loop customer feedback to the business in order to deliver to the customer a more intelligent value proposition'. Customer dialogue is intended to validate and supplement the information that the business already captures about the customer's behaviour and about transactions that take place between the customer and the business. The dialogue process allows the customer to participate in the process of constructing the customer profile that is utilized by the business and allows the customer, where relevant, to evaluate the benefits that are exchanged for their personal information.

Establishing a customer dialogue process is about building trust with the customer through a commitment to greater knowledge of customer needs, which in turn improves the intelligence of the operational, sales and marketing business processes that are used to interact with the customer. In essence, customer dialogue is an agreement with the customer: the customer agrees to provide information that will be used to enhance and customize the service enjoyed by the customer.

At present most businesses use surveillance-based techniques to mine information about customers in an effort to understand or anticipate behaviour. There are three problems with this approach. One is that the information that is available to be analysed for sales and marketing purposes is inadequate and incomplete since it was collected for operational purposes. Secondly, the data available from operational systems is hopelessly fragmented in most businesses and is inconsistent in terms of structure and content, partially incomplete, of variable quality, and in some cases inaccessible. And finally, surveillance-based techniques are distrusted by customers and are correctly seen as an invasion of privacy and abuse of privilege. Having a customer dialogue management layer of software in the enterprise is not intended to substitute for the data warehouse systems that are currently used to analyse customer information. Dialogue data is intended to augment the other data sources in the enterprise and the dialogue process is intended to validate and enhance the process of building customer profiles. In effect, having dialogue allows customers to furnish information about themselves and grant permissions concerning how that data is used.

Traditional market research tended to be performed using (a) personal interviews, or (b) questionnaires that are posted to consumers, or (c) telephone surveys that use cold calling techniques. Personal interviewing tends be very costly and many interviewees are inhibited by the face-to-face contact. Very high numbers of consumers ignore postal surveys and this technique is highly inflexible since the researcher cannot adapt the questionnaire based on earlier answers. Large numbers of consumers decline to participate in telephone surveys, which they tend to find intrusive and inconvenient. In addition, telephone surveys require the respondent to be extremely attentive and can be very cumbersome when they involve multiple response options. In addition to these obstacles to carrying out quality research using traditional means the market researcher has to be continually aware of the non-response error – error introduced by the non-participation of key segments of the market.

An additional problem for most businesses is that different processes in the business capture customer profile information separately as part of the individual operational information systems in the enterprise. Therefore, no control can be exercised over the frequency of customer contact and no standardization can be applied to the customer dialogues that are initiated by the business. An integrated dialogue management system provides the enterprise with a separate discrete layer in the systems architecture of the business to manage dialogues and to intercept all of the processes that launch or initiate dialogues with customers and prospects.

Different processes in the enterprise have separate purposes and these imply different types of interaction with the customer. Current enterprise architectures often confuse these interactions and attempt to locate the information-gathering process as part of multiple operational processes. Market research is still in its infancy on the Internet but it is the fastest growing medium for gathering customer intelligence. The Web is the greatest opportunity ever presented to enterprises for improving the cost-effectiveness of marketing and sales efforts, for forming more productive partnerships with customers, for increasing sales revenues and for increasing profits.

There are a variety of advantages in using the Internet to gain information from consumers and these are listed as follows:[1]

- **Cost effectiveness** The sample size of a market survey on the Internet has little impact on the cost, in marked contrast to the linear relationship between costs and sample size in conventional one-to-one interviewing.

- **Access to elusive segments** The Internet is a more effective means of gaining a response from groups that traditionally have been hard to reach, such as the teenage, single, affluent and well-educated segments.
- **Speed** The results of Internet surveys can immediately be made available for analysis. Survey data can also be readily compared with other online research results.
- **Honesty** The anonymity of the Internet encourages a more frank and candid response by respondents.
- **Location neutrality** The Internet is a very effective means of reaching a geographically dispersed group and facilitates feedback from segments that are not practicable to reach using conventional means.
- **Relationship** Internet market research establishes a relationship with the consumer and allows the consumer to view and update the information provided and allows the researcher to provide feedback to the respondent.
- **Dialogue integration** Conventional market research tended to comprise 'one off' surveys commissioned by different parts of the organization. Internet market research allows all dialogues to be integrated and unified for the entire enterprise.
- **Convenience** Online questionnaires may be completed by the respondent at a time convenient to them in contrast to telephone surveys that have a high level of refusal as they are perceived by consumers to be intrusive and inconvenient.
- **Dynamic** Conventional market research questionnaires tend to comprise a fixed series of questions, where not all questions are relevant to all respondents. Online questionnaires can dynamically reconfigure later questions in response to answered questions.
- **Logical** Internet market research can be structured so that the relevant questions are asked during the course of an online

interaction in contrast to conventional market research that occurs in isolation from the transaction or business event that relates to the research.

For the customer to be placed centre-stage, it is necessary to completely reassess current business intelligence and relationship management models, which amount to customer surveillance, and augment them with a model and a customer interface that guarantees customer control. The conventional data warehouse-type surveillance and analysis of customer behaviour will continue to have a key role in understanding customers, but merely observing customer behaviour cannot fully explain why they behave as they do. In order to fully understand causality – why something happens – requires dialogue between the customer and the business, through which the customer provides feedback to the business.

What consumers want is to be able to register their requirements in a standard format where they exercise control over the information and what it is subsequently used for, and can return to, cancel, or amend the registration details as they wish. The business needs to provide a means of empowering the consumer to become an active participant in the communication process. Thus consumers will impart only the information they wish, and businesses will store only what is provided. It seems more likely that multiple dialogues with multiple suppliers will characterize the nature of future information exchange, but some commentators have suggested that all consumers maintain a single personal 'My Profile' database that could be accessed by preferred suppliers.

Either way, the consumer effectively defines the marketing information application they wish to have provided. In this way, most of the confusion and problems that currently exist in the e-business and marketing intelligence domains disappear.

The failures of business intelligence, relationship marketing and e-commerce all relate to a failure to engage with the customer or to empower the customer to become an active participant in the sales process. Put another way, each of these initiatives can be perceived as a means of exploiting the customer rather than empowering the customer. It follows, therefore, that any attempt to combine these domains in any new initiative will continue to fail unless the customer is put in control of the interaction. For the customer to be placed centre stage it will be necessary to completely displace the current model and replace it with a model that is customer controlled. For this to happen we must design a customer interface that guarantees that the customer is in charge.

The first task to be completed to reverse the existing trend in the market is the design of a conceptual framework that describes how a customer can interact with a supplier, supply information and determine how that information is used. The customer will also define on this intelligent interface the information, messages, promotions, alerts and updates that they wish to receive. And the data that is so captured can be fed directly into a prepackaged database design that can execute the alerts, messages etc. that the customer has defined. The opportunity that exists is to design and construct a comprehensive and tightly integrated environment for customer interaction, which comprises at least the following elements:

- customer registration
- customer contact information
- customer preferences
- customer demographics

- customer psychographics
- customer behaviour (may be linked to transaction systems)
- customer defined alerts
- customer defined update information
- customer defined promotional requests
- customer facility to amend or cancel information
- real-time feedback during customer dialogue.

Those businesses that recognize the potential of the Internet to engage in dialogue with customers will be able to leverage the true potential of the Internet. The shared space can be used to get customer feedback, to engage customers in product co-design, to allow customers to define the customization features they require, to allow customers trade information for benefits and to permit customers to award permissions. The medium also allows businesses to provide feedback, alerts, updates and information services. In short, the medium is best utilized through two-way communication with the quality controls that are enforced by a closed loop communication process. Moving from a world of monologue to a world of dialogue is the basis of relationship building. It also provides the building blocks of business intelligence since, without customer information, there can be no customer differentiation.

The Information Disclosure Compact

When customers disclose information to a supplier (through a business process, in an application form, in a survey) that acquiescence by the customer in the act of freely giving information creates a not unreasonable expectation that the information will be used in future interactions with the customer. Thus, the airline passengers who are asked their meal preferences and indicates that they are vegetarian are going to be more frustrated when they are presented with a non-vegetarian meal than if they had never had their preference canvassed; the hotel guests who state clearly in their loyalty card application that they are non-smokers are going to be more infuriated than usual when they find themselves in a room that has just been vacated by a smoker; and the mobile phone customers who indicate that they are sensitive to price are going to be even more unforgiving if their cellular supplier fails to respond quickly to a competitive pricing deal offered by a competitor. In short, it is dangerous to play at the information game without understanding the consequences. Collecting information and not using it is likely to be counterproductive and damaging to the customer relationship. Toying with an information strategy is potentially catastrophic.

This expectation will become even more intense as more and more enterprises get it right and introduce genuine one-to-one relationships. The customer, in a product-centered relationship with a supplier, has a clear expectation that the business processes are efficient (i.e. that where the customers' requirements fit neatly into the predetermined range of options that are comprehended by 'policy' that the business process will work cleanly) and cheap. The customer who has a one-to-one relationship with a supplier has equally clear expectations that they will enjoy an effective relationship and may be prepared to trade price for convenience or the enhanced quality of the service. By far the worst scenario will be those enterprises that toy with mass customization and create the expectation on the part of the consumer that they are going to enjoy a one-to-one relationship and then fail to deliver on it. By far the best scenario will be those enterprises who manage to deliver a one-to-one relationship and still manage to leverage the synergies of size to offer price competitive products.

Declared Behaviour and Observed Behaviour

An important distinction needs to be clarified between customer preferences and behaviours that are volunteered by the customer in the course of applying for a product or service and the preferences and behaviour demonstrated by that same customer during the course of consuming that product or service. The categories of information assembled from customer declarations typically include personal, demographic and lifestyle data. These details are collected on application forms, questionnaires, evaluations and responses to promotions. While not all of this declared information may be entirely true, what is important is that it is the profile that the customer wishes to have impressed on the supplier. A customer may falsely declare to an airline that he or she is a frequent traveller or inflate their salary to their credit card company or reassure their life insurance provider that they have a healthy exercise regime. There is no evidence that consumers habitually falsify information concerning the actual transaction, since such actions would have legal, contractual and practical consequences. It is in the area of discretionary information, which the recipient has no way of validating, that consumers feel able to exaggerate, mislead or fantasize. And it is precisely this discretionary information that has been the traditional fuel of marketing campaigns. There are many reasons why consumers are cavalier about answering profile-building questions concerning their status and preferences. It may be that consumers feel such questions to be irksome and irrelevant to the transaction. It may also be that consumers find such questions to be intrusive or prurient. Some proportion of consumers may feel that, in providing personal information, the safest course is to supply answers that are deemed to be reassuring to the company seeking the information. The principal explanation for all of these reactions is the absence of a tangible link between (a) providing information and (b) receiving benefits. Consumers are aware that there must be some purpose in asking these questions, but they are not at all sure what that purpose is. Certainly, in their commercial intercourse with the supplier (who has been armed with this information) there is rarely any sign that this information is being used to personalize the interaction between supplier and customer. And, in the absence of any evidence to the contrary, some consumers will conclude that the information may be used to disadvantage the customer. In a commercial universe where every act of communication by the consumer is a dead end, the communication process itself becomes debased and, ultimately, redundant. Across a large part of the market this has occurred.

Behavioural information, in marked contrast to declared information, describes records of fact. Each telephone call, credit card transaction, bank withdrawal or sales transaction is a verifiable real-world event. The data that represents the record of these events is reasonably verifiable and can be assembled into useful nuggets of information that provide insights concerning the customer. It is here in the domain of observed behaviour that the marketing focus has been fixed during the course of the past decade. The greater part of the investment in business intelligence systems is centred on the capture, integration and analysis of customer transaction records. In the earlier data warehouse projects (from 1990 to 1995) there was a tendency to construct massive databases of customer information and to subject the data to ad hoc analysis in search of nuggets of intelligence. In recent years, the accumulated wisdom of the early adopters has been distilled into a suite of analytical applications that present a structured analysis of retention, risk, sales, promotions, segmentation, satisfaction and profitability to the business. The application of highly technical analytical techniques to distil propensity models of customer behaviour has proven extremely successful and has shifted marketing from a product focus to a customer focus and from art to science. This has been a laudable advance but, as we take stock after a decade of development, a number of dangerous deficiencies are evident.

There are challenges in achieving the complete integration of the data because it is a technically complex undertaking. There are problems of maintaining the integration of customer data as companies engage in disposals, mergers and takeovers that continually create new data fragmentation. There is the problem that customer analysis is stuck in a rut of planning and control rather than service enhancement. There is the problem of distinguishing between individual and household and between customer and appliance. There is the problem of accommodating permission marketing principles into a process that is largely hidden from view. There is the problem of placating privacy advocates and regulators who are seeking constraints on the degree of surveillance of customer behaviour that is tolerated. And then there is the principal problem and it is the same problem that arises with declared data. Namely that there is generally no connection, from the consumers' perspective, between the information that is captured and the quality of the value proposition that is subsequently on offer. This prohibition on customer participation and the disconnect between the value of what is traded by the consumer and the value of what is received in turn goes to the heart of the impending crisis in marketing and must, sooner or later, be addressed.

Underestimating the Information Feedback Loop

A feature of product design and deployment in recent times is the extent to which the consumer is involved in the validation process. This does not suggest that the consumer is an active participant in the design process nor is the consumer's role confined to the responsive format of focus groups. It is simply the case that companies are prepared to launch products that are well short of being fully functional, on the basis that early adapters in the market will be willing to test the product and identify enhancements. A good example can be found in the market for consumer software. Many software releases, particularly upgrades to products already owned by the customer, contain an extraordinarily high number of bugs. The commercial rationale for this behaviour is that the users will test the product to destruction far faster than any internal testing process and therefore, the speed with which the product can reach the market and be perfected is much faster than perfecting it before releasing it to the market. This feedback process assumes the existence of a cadre of consumers who are early adapters of new software releases and relies on the willingness of these customers to take on this role. This practice now extends to a wide variety of product innovations outside of the technology domain and can be seen in partial releases of financial service products, recreational products and appliances.

There is now strong and growing evidence that businesses that have large numbers of detractors (i.e. dissatisfied customers) are experiencing sharp business decline and it can also be demonstrated that businesses experiencing growth have a high number of promoters (i.e. satisfied customers that would recommend the company to others).[2] It is not likely that this was always the case. For a long time customer satisfaction indices were trivialized by management teams that were well aware that there had never been a strong correlation between customer satisfaction and company performance. Despite the global usage of the standard American Customer Satisfaction Index (ACSI) it has always been a struggle to demonstrate how satisfaction surveys add value to business processes or the bottom line. It is difficult not to conclude that this change is attributable to the increased bandwidth of an information society that is now available to consumers to broadcast their grievances.

A Charter for Consumers

The following principles describe the consents and prohibitions which afford protection to consumers who, in the course of their relationship with a supplier, make personal and behavioural data available to that supplier. These principles, when adhered to, will signal a willingness on the part of the supplier to treat the customer as an individual, utilize all data made available by the consumer to improve any product or service offering and to engage only in meaningful and personalized communications with that customer.

Consumers should use these principles as a guide to the level of personalized relationship that exists between them and any supplier. Consumers should note that many suppliers do not capture customer information or advertise themselves as seeking to build relationships with customers and, obviously, such suppliers cannot be judged according to these principles.

Suppliers should be aware that an implicit contract exists between supplier and consumer and where a supplier collects consumer data the consumer is entitled to the protection of their privacy and, in instances where the customer volunteers information about themselves, to a satisfactory return for making this asset available.

- **Privacy** The consumers' data will at all times be protected and secured by the supplier and will comply with all legislative and statutory protections, prohibitions and guarantees as are in force in the jurisdiction of residence of the consumer.

- **Protection** The consumer will be protected from unsolicited material from third parties and customer details will, in no circumstances, be made available to any party other than the entity granted the data by the consumer, including any subsidiary or associated companies of the company that holds the data. In addition, the supplier will not take any data from a third party or a published source without the knowledge and permission of the consumer.

- **Utilization** The consumer will, in return for making information available to the supplier, be assured that this information will be utilized for the purposes of improving the value proposition or service or product offering of the supplier.

- **Personalization** The consumer will, in return for making personal data available to the supplier, be entitled to a personalized service and personalized communications.

- **Control** The relationship between the consumer and supplier will, at all times, be under the control of the consumer with regard to information disclosed, communications received and services promoted. The supplier will acknowledge that the nature of the relationship will, at all times, be determined and controlled by the consumer.

- **Permission** The consumer may alter, change or otherwise update or amend any information held about them. In addition, the consumer may control the flow of information from the supplier and will always be empowered to select or deselect those communications or category of communications that they wish to receive from the supplier.

- **Transparency** The consumer will at all times be able to view the profile of the consumer held by the supplier and will be able to view any alerts that the supplier has prescribed to respond to that consumer in specific circumstances.

- **Exchange** The supplier will at all times indicate, in terms satisfactory to the consumer, the improvements in service that will accrue from any specific data disclosure.
- **Termination** The consumer may withdraw any or all rights granted to the supplier and the supplier will delete all discretionary information held about the individual.
- **Probity** The consumer will be entitled to know that the supplier is adhering to the principles that underpin the relationship and the supplier will permit accredited agencies to monitor and audit their processes.

Consumer Motivation

The engagement process that is facilitated by the customer registration process is designed to benefit discerning consumers. The benefits to the consumer of participating in a dialogue with the supplier include the following:

- **Engagement** Most consumers wish to combat the alienation that is a feature of most relationships in the consumer to business market. Engagement builds long-term relationships and facilitates a two-way communication process between supplier and consumer. Frequent users will particularly value this facility since it provides a formal basis for communication. The consumer can register their preferences as well as record their grievances. In this way the user can evaluate whether the supplier values their custom; if the supplier listens to their point of view it demonstrates that they are genuinely dedicated to building relationships with individual customers.
- **Authorization** In a business environment that increasingly values confidentiality and privacy it is necessary for supplier and consumer to combat distrust and to provide a transparent basis

for doing business. Most consumers are vaguely aware that their rights to privacy may not be protected in all instances by suppliers and that many unsolicited (and often unwelcome) promotions are directed at the consumer. This process will provide a basis for the consumer to authorize permissions across a range of activities.

- **Currency** In every relationship information and circumstances change over time and the registration process allows the consumer to update their own personal data as well as providing the opportunity to update preferences, permissions and profiles.

- **Validation** Suppliers constantly observe consumer behaviour and make assumptions about the requirements and profiles of their customers. Sometimes these assumptions are based on unsound premises or on incomplete information. By publishing the consumer profile information to the individual consumer it provides a basis for the consumer to validate or to query any of these underlying assumptions that guide the business relationship.

- **Personalization** Every consumer who has a relationship with a business, based on repeat purchases or a long-term relationship, will wish to have their own requirements and preferences reflected in a personalized service. This might be reflected in a customization of product, service, channel, or price. A two-way dialogue that ensures that all communications from the supplier are relevant to the consumer can only satisfy the consumer demand for one-to-one relationships.

- **Control** In a business relationship where there is no feedback it is not possible for the consumer to exert influence or control over the business relationship and it is not possible for the supplier to optimize the business processes to satisfy their customers. The feedback loop provided by the Registration process provides the consumer with a means of influencing the nature of the relationship as well as influencing product directions and the business strategy of the enterprise.

Conclusions

It used to be that customers were the spoils of war but now they have become active participants. The role of the Internet as a shared space for collaborating with customers is a potential that has yet to be realized. As a medium it provides a compelling opportunity for customization, co-design, feedback and exchange. Consumers are able to register their profile details using the consumer profile questionnaire, which complies with a Customer Charter, ensuring that checks and balances are put in place as required by the consumer with regard to their privacy and the confidentiality of their profile data. The consumer may register details concerning preferences, interests, activities, orientations and requirements. Consumers need disclose only those details they wish, in order to improve the quality of service they receive. The Internet annihilates distinctions that used to matter a great deal. The Net blurs the distinction between product and service; test marketing and marketing; market research and customer feedback; brand advertising and promotion; content and transaction. As these distinctions shrivel into insignificance, the urgency of the fundamental question intensifies: How should we use our technologies to create and manage closer, durable relationships with our customers?

This does not mean that the majority of consumers do not value dialogue; it merely means that customers have not been sufficiently exposed to the benefits of dialogue in such a way that it has become a conditioned expectation and automatic consumer demand. The distorting factor that creates much of the disillusionment is the monologue that emanates from suppliers masquerading as a two-way communication. Of course, we should not neglect to observe that a minority of suppliers are proceeding diligently on the road to mass customized services and communications but, as has been explored at greater length already in this book, there is no evidence of a flight from mass marketing to mass customization.

The implications for marketing appear, on a cursory examination, to be obvious. People can now be bombarded all the time with campaigns and invitations and the goal will be to get the right messages to the right people. The result will be a screaming demand for profiles.

8
The New Practice of Marketing

From Selling to Buying

The Myth of Perpetual Turbulence

A considerable period has elapsed since Philip Kotler, the renowned marketing guru, drew a distinction between STP marketing (segmenting, targeting and positioning) and LGD marketing (lunch, golf and dinner). Despite his warning that the mass market was dissolving into hundreds of micromarkets, a new science of marketing has been slow to emerge. The traditional marketing manager is like a pilot who takes to the skies with some simple navigation equipment. He can determine altitude, airspeed and direction. He knows only his next destination. And every natural disorder is treated as turbulence. Managers are prized that can deal with the turbulence calmly and effectively. In a world where 'discontinuities, irregularities, and volatilities seem to be proliferating rather than diminishing',[1] those few who have finely honed instincts for the mood of the moment are always at a premium. At its best this approach to marketing relies on leadership, creativity, insight, even genius. But it is not science. So what kind of marketing manager do we need when we can understand and anticipate most of the threats and opportunities. In effect, what kind of manager do we need in a world without turbulence? This may seem like a strange proposition having earlier argued that we are experiencing unprecedented change. But the end of a particular category of chaos is in sight.

The element of chance is fast disappearing in the decision-making process. The existence of customer profiles dramatically alters the levels of uncertainty. The essence of good judgement is the ability to evaluate known facts and then to exercise intuition to fill the gaps of the unknown and dark places. The risk inherent in any decision lies in the assumptions being made by the decision maker. In the past these assumptions were, predominantly, assumptions about facts that we did not know or could not establish for certain. Increasingly, the assumptions will be about our interpretations of complete knowledge about the problem. Those who survive the transition into the age of certainty will all be playing with marked decks of cards. The art of management will never be quite the same again.

Because of the immense difficulty of 'knowing' what the optimum decision is in any set of circumstances, we tended, in the past, to create security by clinging tenaciously to those few things that we do know with some certainty. The fact that these few brush strokes of information were but a fragment of the picture that we need to see did not deter most mass marketing executives. The chances that these few strands of intelligence might amount to a basis for determining a course of action might have been remote but, since the alternative was permanent paralysis, we strove to rationalize our decision making with reference to the few precious facts at our disposal. Thus the worlds of advertising and branding are more often focused on the sublime rather than the empirical. After all, if we are persuaded that the buying behaviour of customers is impenetrable then there will be a natural tendency to regard the whole process as an art form that defies scientific analysis. And so the conventional marketing mind turns away from empirical analysis to vaguer concepts that defy measurement.

It is clear that recent decades have wrought fundamental changes in the patterns of communication in general between government and citizen, supplier and customer and consumer and market. The combined pattern of these changes tends to suggest a replacement of existing models that are participative, intuitive and personal, with a new model that is representational, rational and remote. The citizens express themselves through polls rather than at democratically convened meetings. The customers express themselves through their purchasing behaviour and challenge suppliers to keep up with their profile. The consumer communicates preference and propensity by declaring allegiance to personal value systems that dictate lifestyle and fashion choices. Ultimately the advertising agency, the nationwide retailer and the political pollster are all in pursuit of the same thing – profiles, profiles, profiles.

This general tendency is reasonably well established and many commentators argue the downside of these trends. It will be pointed out that a society driven by remote polling mechanisms will result in policies that are shortlived, fickle, anonymous, brutal and capable of endless manipulation. The alternative interpretation is that it is democratic, responsive, accurate, sophisticated and empowering of the many social subcultures that have traditionally been obscured in the homogenous mass. It is not relevant to ask, for the purposes of this book, if it is a good or a bad thing or what it means in the wider sociopolitical context. Also, it is clearly melodramatic to declare that it has actually happened. But it requires a wilful blindness not to acknowledge that it is in the process of happening and there is no evidence that it will be reversed.

As usual when we find ourselves at a crossroads in the development of an idea we should seek clarity on the way forward by attempting to identify the apparent contradictions in the system that has evolved to date. That has been a significant motivation in writing this book and I will take time here to summarize these apparent contradictions.

- There is the overarching contradiction that divides the advocates of personalization and homogenization.
- There is the inherent contradiction that is perceived between disembodied technology and personalization – the 'high-tech, low-touch' syndrome.
- There is the tension between customer lifetime measures of performance and those measures that derive from recency, frequency and monetary value.
- There is the contradiction between merely having data and claiming to have information.
- There is the contradiction between having personalization messaging capabilities and not having personalization intelligence capabilities.
- There is the contradiction between enhanced service customization and the protection of consumer privacy.
- There is the tension between message volume and message quality.
- There is also the contradiction between the desire to increase convenience while at the same time increasing the level of anxiety through over stimulation.
- There is the contradiction between being guided by customers in the design of value propositions and the need for radical product innovation that is beyond the horizon of customer perception.
- And then there is the really big contradiction between claiming to engage in dialogue when, in reality, there is really only monologue.

Consumers too are struggling with what appear to be contradictions. Consider the common consumer mantras such as 'If I get any more junk mail I'm going to scream!' or 'If my personal information is being used without my permission, I'm going to sue!' (all suggesting a demand for greater protection). Contrast these with the equally common consumer reactions of 'If you ask me that question again I'm going to cry!' or 'If you cannot anticipate my requirements I'm going to leave' (suggesting a demand for greater personalization).

In fact, there is no contradiction at all. The entire paradox is resolved by the single expedient of transferring control of the business relationship to the consumer. In circumstances where the consumer selects what personal information they will disclose, what benefits they will enjoy, what stimulation they wish to be exposed to and what marketing messages they wish to receive, the paradox evaporates. Customer control will need to extend to the withdrawal of information as well as the selection of message frequency, interval and channel. The task of the marketing department is to provide the technical and business infrastructure to facilitate and empower this interaction. Competitive advantage will rest with those who offer the richest interaction environment and, by so doing, establish an unrivalled level of intelligence about the market they operate in and an unprecedented level of trust with their customers.

The challenge that this scenario presents to traditional marketing departments is that, to participate in a world where success depends on the design and innovation of complex systems, the marketing person needs to be competent to truly 'own' these systems. It is no longer sufficient to rely on the competency of the IT department to drive innovation in the business or for marketing visionaries with no real conception of how information is managed to specify systems that technology is incapable of delivering. The gap that exists in most organizations between marketing and IT has two negative consequences. The first is that the organization is forced to rely on the business intuition of technologists to spot opportunities in the data. The second is that marketers will never fully endorse what they do not truly understand. Where success has been experienced in harnessing technology to business opportunity it has usually been the result of having technologists who happen to have an acute knowledge of the business or marketers who happen to be technology enthusiasts. In other words, it is the result of happenstance.

In the past, the marketing function was persuaded that it was responsible for managing the 'exchange relationship' where exchange was assumed to be the exchange of a product for payment. Therefore, it naturally follows that where the exchange transaction now requires information to flow in both directions the marketing function would recognize its responsibility to ensure that a satisfactory information exchange relationship also exists. It is abundantly clear that the marketing function has, thus far, failed to take decisive ownership of this crucial aspect of the business/consumer relationship. Some crude solutions to this dilemma have been attempted by organizations. The most common is to rotate IT and marketing personnel between their respective departments. This often leads to some positive outcomes but is a superficial solution. The usual politics of stovepiped organizations results in a good deal of suspicion at having a 'cuckoo' in the camp and most professionals will gravitate back to the familiar surroundings of their own discipline as soon as a defined project is completed. Even in circumstances where a senior executive with the necessary authority merges the technology and business missions, the benefits wrought by such efforts rarely outlast the departure of the individual. It is all too common to witness dramatic innovations in companies only to later observe these firms lapse back into their programmed modes of behaviour. The corporate organization is like a wobbly blancmange; it is capable of considerable temporary flexibility but when the external pressure is removed it will unfailingly return to its original moulded shape.

The solution lies in reshaping the organizational structure entirely and many of the e-commerce start-ups that have survived have managed to successfully avoid the traditional demarcations that bedevil the more established businesses. But the logic of the information wars also demands that the business disciplines that reside in the new structures are reshaped. It is a fact that most of the innovations in marketing in recent decades are being driven by technological developments that reside outside of the formal discipline. And it is not simply a matter of merging the disciplines of marketing and information technology; this simplistic solution would result in a most peculiar hybrid. There are many aspects of information technology that the marketing function does not need to be aware of and there are aspects of other disciplines such as law, ethics, psychology, human factor analysis, artificial intelligence, pattern analysis and statistics that do need to be included. Many academics tasked with producing marketing graduates readily accept the critique presented here and are attempting to address the existing deficit. The result will be a very different kind of syllabus than that which previous generations of marketing graduates have known. The systematic study of the discipline of customer satisfaction may be perceived to be less glamorous than concocting alluring brand strategies for mass advertising. But brand managers are themselves only too aware that, with a fragmented media already meeting the focused needs of a segmented market, there are now fewer and fewer outlets for mass advertising. Mass network television audiences have shrunk in the face of advances by video, cable, satellite and the Internet. In the 20 years from 1980 to 2000, when the number of television households in the US increased by more than 20%, peak audiences for top sitcom shows decreased by 25%. In circumstances where content is increasingly customized and is capable of leaking into the market through a variety of channels, it is no longer the case that the medium is the message. The message is now independent of the medium.

The fact that a major transition is taking place does not suggest the end of history. But it does suggest that, with the crystallization of the new model, there will be a slowing down of turbulence and a prolonged period of consolidation. And so we have reached the endgame. And, as with chess, victory goes to the player who makes the next-to-last mistake.[2] While the past decade has been littered with a variety of mistakes from which we can recover, the final game-losing mistake is to draw back from the logic of engaging the customer as a sovereign subject rather than a docile object. And acceptance of this reality requires, perforce, that the entire edifice of mass marketing collapses. Endgames in chess are characterized by defensive and positional manoeuvrings by the players until one achieves even a slight advantage that allows them to go on the offensive. It can often be a tedious business as one player waits for the other to make a slight mistake and tilt the balance. The ultimate resolution of this impasse will occur when, either (a) customers will expose their profile and requirements for marketing in a controlled environment, or (b) all of the businesses in a particular sector will be combined in a directory where they all expose their product catalogues to be contrasted and compared. Both supplier and customer have been slow to place their information cards on the table. For suppliers there has seemed to be good reason for timidity. Information transparency may lead to conditions of near-perfect competition which would result in a commercial bloodbath with unpredictable consequences. Despite the fact that the technological means has been available for some time, few businesses have been prepared to take the first step towards the brink but all are aware that, sooner or later in one business after another, a competitor will do so. And when that happens, the final moves on the chessboard will happen quickly and decisively. Information advantage alone may not win the day, but it is set to be the differentiating factor that will determine the final outcome.

Revising Perceptions of Customer Interaction

Part of the difficulty in devising a new science of marketing is the need to completely redefine the nature of the relationship that exists between business and consumer. This will be the radical breakthrough that we have been waiting for and will transform the potential of information technology by providing clarity and focus that is missing today. The new definition is going to have to transfer the initiative for the transmission of marketing messages from the business to the customer. And we can expect a strong rearguard action to be fought by traditionalists who have only ever been accountable for business results rather than customer service, who have always been encouraged to achieve short term gains even at the expense of long term value and who are accustomed to a culture of customer exploitation rather than personalization.

And this transformation will occur, not because it is a good or ethical thing or because it is promoted by advocates or legislators, but because it is the inescapable logic of the technology. It is naïve to assume that technology is neutral and can be harnessed to a range of different visions. In much the same way that the pervasive technologies of the late nineteenth century (e.g. railways, mass print media, wireless broadcasting) provided the cement to bind the nation state, the technologies of the late 20th century (e.g. air travel, Internet, satellite television) provide the solvents that are dissolving the nation state.

Conversely, the modern economics of information and customization allows small groups, at the subnational level, to be recognized and accommodated more easily than was the case in an era of standardized mass production. So too it is with business. The technologies of the early and mid-20th century replaced craftsmanship and intimacy with standardization and alienation. Mass marketing was the appropriate response to, and a driver of, the emergence of a mass consumer culture. The 21st century is characterized by atomization as individual channels of communication are available to and from every consumer and mass marketing will be sundered in the process.

Individually controlled devices can only be controlled by the individual in possession of the device. All messages transmitted to an individually owned device must be intended only for the recipient. There is no possibility that individuals will permit themselves to be controlled remotely by such devices. There is no likelihood that the technology can be ignored or uninvented. We cannot return to the primitive state of broadcasting to an undifferentiated mass. We cannot, within any timescale we can comprehend, foresee a time when such devices will be biologically implanted. The individual customer has, for the foreseeable future, seized control. All resistance is futile.

The first step that businesses must take is to recognize that the customer interaction of the future will be fundamentally different. The shift that is taking place is moving the model away from one that pushes products to customers and towards a model that empowers customers to pull the products and services that they need. In such an environment the service component that needs to be embedded in the interaction will be much more important as a differentiator. Understanding what the customer wants, responding to the individual's life events and facilitating the collapse of time will all be crucial elements in the matrix of competitive advantage. It is highly likely that one important consequence of this shift in thinking will be a radical rationalization and reorganization of the market. For example, it makes little sense to a consumer that health care insurance and health care provision are separate processes. Likewise it is a nuisance to a consumer to have to purchase a travel product and travel insurance separately. It is not inconceivable that a mortgage provider would provide a furniture removal facility or even a school enrolment facility for their customers. Once we begin to associate information with processes in a logical manner we frequently unmask peculiarities and odd inefficiencies in the process under observation. This will act as an impetus to 'think out of the box'. Remember that a business process is not complete 'until the last aspect of the final outcome is complete from the point of view of the person who initiates the process'.[3] And, in business, it is only the customer who is vested with the authority to initiate a transaction process. Therefore, it is from the perspective of the customer that the process must be considered. For example, only from the confines of a very blinkered perspective can the act of buying an airline ticket be considered a real customer process. Going on vacation or taking a business trip; these are customer processes.

The evolution of a new cognitive model has been slow and laboured because of the inherent assumption that we do not or cannot know all the factors that collectively determine an outcome in the market. Or because, even armed by the information, we continue, instead of trying to identify the patterns that are there, to seek to validate existing hypotheses based on preconceived recognizable patterns. This approach to process innovation creates cycles of uncertainty as we take one step forward, then two steps back, before proceeding again. Since the advent of business intelligence technologies the marketing function has been mired in this confusion and perceives itself as oscillating between 'the soft intuitive perspective of the customer-driven school and the hard, shareholder or profit-driven perspective'.[4] But, in reality, the only choice that actually exists concerns the timing of the transformation to a customer-led model and, in the course of the transition, momentous adjustments will be made to shareholder value on a global scale. What has delayed the orderly transition to customer-centred commerce *en masse* has been a failure to understand the nature of the transformation that is occurring. Information is perceived to be a new ingredient in the ongoing process of customer manipulation instead of comprehending that it is the new currency of exchange.

The Italian philosopher, Umberto Eco, in his acclaimed book, *Serendipities*, explores the reasons why so many projects that began in error ended in success. Columbus attempting to circumnavigate the globe and discovering America instead is the most obvious case in point. The problem is that we have difficulty in altering our cognitive models when planning for or experiencing real change. Our perception map is incomplete and we seek to identify new things by scanning existing things in our memory bank for a match. The problem for the 21st century manager is that too many novel phenomena are crowding in and no integrating framework exists to make immediate sense of it all. More crucially, even where existing phenomena are understood there is the problem of anticipating and comprehending each new one. The most egregious business misconception that has been explored at length in this book is the continued treatment of information age customers as if they were anonymous units of a mass market. Eco notes that when Marco Polo encountered a rhinoceros he assumed it was a unicorn since he had heard of the unicorn (a fictitious animal) but had not heard of the rhinoceros (a real animal). Eco wryly observes that 'the real problem of a critique of our own cultural models is to ask, when we see a unicorn, if by any chance it is not a rhinoceros'.[5] As we survey the scarred landscape where the information wars currently rage, it is hard not to draw the conclusion that many of the participants are in full pursuit of the unicorn.

As the mass market atomizes into its individual units of consumption the real challenge will be to recast the relationship between business and consumer. Many observers insist on believing that the existing business structure can absorb these requirements without needing fundamental change. It is argued that the basic business process can be easily adapted to accommodate customization and that technology can be easily adopted to facilitate it. But this analysis misses a fundamental point about the way in which individualization must operate. In the 'old' business process the ownership of the entire process – responsibility, authority and the work performed – all are vested inside the organization. In the 'new' business process only responsibility for honouring the contract between business and consumer will be located within the organization. The work actually performed will, in most instances, be subcontracted elsewhere and, crucially, authority over the process will be vested in the consumer.

It is important to realize, when we speak of the massive increase in customer information available to businesses, that consumers also have more information. When today's consumer goes shopping for an item they have available to them a plethora of information about competing products that would have been unimaginable to a previous generation. In addition to the information that can be gleaned from the websites of suppliers there are a wide variety of information intermediaries and regulatory agencies which help consumers to contrast, compare and evaluate products. And consumers do, of course, share and test the results of their evaluations with one another. This process of independent evaluation is considerably more efficient than trawling through the masses of largely irrelevant marketing information that clogs up their letterboxes and e-mail inboxes. The process of 'selling' is, in actual fact, giving way to a process of 'buying'. Increasingly the goal of marketing will be to attract buyers rather than to promote products. This fact is calculated to fundamentally alter the balance of power in the relationship between consumer and supplier.

Resolving the Information Paradox

The last decade has seen two major technological offensives that were directed at improving knowledge of, and intimacy with, customers. One, the business intelligence drive to achieve an integrated view of the customer has been a qualified success but has left an astonishingly high level of disappointments in its wake. The second, e-business, has emerged as a radical and permanent feature of the market but not without having precipitated a bloodbath for investors and businesses that was unprecedented in the history of applying technology to business. The fact is that both of these initiatives were pursued in a fragmented way without, in many cases, any clear idea about the potential benefits. Participation in both these waves of innovation was driven less by a coherent understanding of benefits than by an instinct that these were important milestones in the age of information. This 'fear of being left behind' by early innovators all point to a debilitating absence of strategy in the customer management process. The reason why the goal of automating the relationship with customers has been so difficult to achieve, compared to the financial, manufacturing, logistics or personnel functions of the enterprise, is explained by the absence of a coherent agreed process map of the customer management function. In other words, in many businesses there is no stable customer management process at all. The relationship of business to suppliers, investors, employees and government is reasonably stable and well-defined. The question 'what is it precisely that we are seeking to automate?' has not been at all as clear when we are dealing with customers.

In the past, in business, causality didn't matter. It was enough to know that there was a close correlation between two different phenomena (e.g. when demand increases, prices rise) and businesses could derive benefit from knowing about it. The reason for the association was sometimes obvious but more often was the subject of widely held assumptions. Many of these assumptions we now know to be wrong (e.g. when the demand for innovative and expensive new technologies increases, prices fall). We have now reached a stage where it is not tenable to simply assert an assumption or a range of competing speculations that could neither be proven nor unproven. Now we have reached a stage where it is possible, and necessary, to know why an association exists. The strategy of exploiting information is steadily shifting from one of observing the market (and reacting to changes) toward one that seeks to influence and redefine the market. The business objective is no longer merely to adapt to the external environment, but to modify it.

The anxiety and confusion experienced by information-poor businesses that are paralysed by the absence of customer intelligence is, in many instances, matched by those information-rich businesses that are paralysed by the complexity of the information. In circumstances where the amount of stored corporate data doubles every two years there is a limit to the ability of companies to extract meaningful customer intelligence from this ever-expanding mass. Ultimately the question 'what information do we have?' must be replaced by the more pertinent question 'what information do we need?' Only then will businesses realize that the key to real intelligence lies in the acquisition of meaningful customer data rather than endlessly analysing the data that happens to be available. This is not to suggest that much of the data that is captured at present as a by-product of transaction processes is not useful for marketing purposes, but total reliance on such data leads to a business rationality that is bounded by those existing processes.

One important feature of the past number of decades of computer development is that we have witnessed no real discontinuity in the way that human beings behave. The power of technology has been most successfully employed when it has been harnessed to existing modes of behaviour. This has the twin results of accelerating the adaptation of the technology as well as retarding its potential. A consensus has been growing for some time in the information technology community that this is about to change. Increasingly, there is speculation that advances in computer and communication technology will precipitate a radical discontinuity in human history.[6]

The transitions from data to information or from product to customer or from tangible to intangible do not rank as radical discontinuities in human history, however dramatic and painful they appear to those organizations enduring change. These are early tremors in a landscape braced for more dramatic events. A market that merely sells more products faster does not alter the essential fundamentals of the existing consumer-producer relationship. An average day in the life of a brand manager has not changed much at all in the past several decades. In fact, the marketing function generally has been the least impacted, until now, by new technology. This observation alone demonstrates that the basic business proposition has not been altered by technology, however much the technology has revolutionized every aspect of production and distribution. We live in a world where technology is omnipresent but where most aspects of consumer commerce remain reassuringly familiar. Because the benefits generated by technology are internally focused on ordering, stock taking, book keeping and distribution, the technology tends to remain invisible to the consumer. We are still driven by needs; we satisfy those needs by assessing competing options, make a selection decision, pay for the product and receive a receipt. And yet the fact remains that, 'for the first time in centuries, it is simply impossible today to imagine the world that our children will live in'.[7]

The Disintegrating Enterprise and Random Acts of Marketing

When one looks at the root causes of individual corporate failures there tends to be a limited range of possibilities to explain the pattern of decline. Either the expressed corporate strategy was deeply flawed (rare, but not unheard of) or the corporate strategy was basically sound, but was blindsided to some significant external trend that was identified too late (much more common) or the corporation had too many divergent corporate strategies generating confusion and dissonance (all too common). If faced with a selection problem, we have many options to choose from, but only one optimum solution; success lies in selecting the optimum solution quickly. In situations based on reality there is only ever a binary outcome: survival or elimination. The failure to recognize this reality arises from the existence of a number of fallacies that are commonly encountered in marketing strategies.

The first is the fallacy of asymmetry whereby a marketing strategy contains a hodgepodge of marketing approaches that are diverse and contradictory. There is a well established history during the past decade of organizations giving sponsorship to contradictory areas like relationship, branding, advertising, promotion and pricing policies all at the same time. Businesses skip from being product-led to customer-led and back again just as quickly as they morph from being socially responsible to being socially indifferent. This absence of any intellectual rigour is plainly unsustainable.

The second is the fallacy of approximation. The idea that there are degrees of fitness in any strategy and that survival can be achieved simply by not selecting a horrendous choice of strategy misses the point. In a classroom or seminar context degrees of excellence can be ascribed to competing policy alternatives. Survival simply depends on not selecting a totally inappropriate policy or strategy. Reality is different. The number of competing options is infinite. And there is only one optimum route to ensure survival. The company that comes closest wins. It is a simple yardstick. All mass marketing strategies are based on the discovery of common denominators that can be used to approximate the market. As the discovery of meaningful common denominators becomes more difficult, approximation will cease to be useful.

The third is the fallacy of sampling. There are two things wrong with focus groups. Firstly, simply by being readily available to participate, the representative sample is anything but representative. Because of the variety and complexity of the market it is extraordinarily difficult to draw valid generalizations from a small sample that can be confidently applied to the whole. And secondly, the product manager sponsoring the focus group has a product, strategy or career to protect. The outcomes of focus groups are often disappointing. A focus group can react to a pilot TV show and indicate a preference but a focus group would never have originated *Star Trek*. Now it might reasonably be claimed that they were never intended to do so but the reality is that they have become an intrinsic part of the product design process for consumer products (just as user groups have become for business products) and they are speaking on behalf of an increasingly baffled public.[8]

It has been observed that the most successful technologies are the ones that have become ubiquitous and undetectable. Our usage of many common objects such as the telephone, the ATM machine or the fax machine are not perceived as high technology by the billions of users that take such systems for granted. There is no substantial skill required to utilize such devices and there is no mystique associated with the most pervasive, and thus the most successful, technologies. We cannot claim that the use of telephones, faxes, ATMs or even the PC peaked because there was a more technologically literate population available for such equipment, although the levels of educational attainment did rise substantially in the core markets for these products. The reality is that these products transfer effortlessly to populations with a far lower level of educational attainment. And any assumption for the adoption of any new technology that rests on increased technological literacy is based on an unsubstantiated premise. The technology has to be more and more sophisticated in order that its usage is more and more intuitive.

Wireless devices as we know them today are bandwidth constrained, ergonomically constrained, device constrained and comfort constrained and will remain so in the near term. The proposition that users will enthusiastically engage with such devices to access information sources is unreasonable. However, the proposition that such devices will act on the user by transmitting information is entirely reasonable. The use of software agents who represent the consumer by interacting with the information universe is a far safer assumption. Therefore, we return to the distinction between data and information and must now consider the potential of a knowledge-processing universe where embedded intelligence is made available to users so that the device, whatever we ultimately decide to call it, will become a real time alerting device rather than a user interface.

Significant shifts in the underlying technology infrastructure usually solve problems that we are aware of within the boundaries of our cognitive framework (what we understand to be the intelligence building process) and the perception field (what we are capable of perceiving as inputs to the intelligence building process). Thus, new technologies typically solve familiar problems and only late in the day do we find a real use for such capabilities. This is when the transformation shift occurs. In effect, the real value of new technological capabilities is that they serve to expand the perception field and create the potential for more integrated and more intensive cognitive processes to be realized. As real time knowledge-push applications materialize we will know that the transformation is upon us.

A frequent excuse for the relatively low level of sustained commitment to the business transformation required to create real relationships is that the technology does not work, is not yet mature or that the task of constructing the kind of integrated information technology infrastructure is too complex for many organizations. This technology excuse does not stand any scrutiny. The complexity of defining the business rules for relationship marketing and the radical transformation in business processes and culture provides a more persuasive line of enquiry. It is clear that the early adopters in the field were usually champions of the concept who were capable of building a communication bridge across the yawning gulf that separated the marketing and technology functions of the organization. This was no easy task and these heroic individuals who unmasked the potential of information during the past decade are described by John McKean in his book *Information Masters* as 'a handful of visionary individuals who turned up at the right place but at the wrong time (twenty years too soon). . . and feel a personal calling to attack this dysfunction against monumental odds'.[9] The absence of a clearly defined job role to take command of the information resource is a key part of the explanation. The term Chief Information Officer (CIO) was always a misleading title and merely described the head of the technology function. The reality is that the pioneers of customer intelligence were very often gifted generalists who were capable of bridging the gap between strategy, process and technology. It is certainly a complex undertaking. But no dramatic breakthrough can be anticipated until the need for an information exploitation specialization is more widely recognized.

Conclusions

The information wars are now approaching the end game; albeit that the end game may be messy and protracted. The value of information, the role of technology, the collapse of time and space and mass affluence are all acknowledged drivers in the inexorable advance of individualization. But, ultimately, it is the failure to acknowledge the role of the consumer that is now hampering progress. The current challenge is not to help businesses deploy the technology that they need. It is not even to help them to acquire the information they need. It is to help them to overcome the intellectual challenge of devising business applications that will allow customers to exchange information for benefits in an environment of trust that operates for the mutual satisfaction of both customer and business.

Therefore, it is likely that the next and penultimate phase will be one of considerable flux where different and conflicting paths will be followed by businesses. There may be a temporary and unsustainable split in the market between businesses offering price and those offering service differentiators. The commercial environment may be reshaped by a clearer distinction between those firms that own customer relationships and those firms that manufacture consumer products. The privacy debate will oscillate between restrictions and freedoms before a mature consumer activism asserts itself. Many businesses will hedge their bets by attempting to back both product and customer strategies, but this will result in a nugatory organizational dysfunction that will ultimately force a clear choice. The costs associated with managing and storing information will tumble and eliminate many of the cost-benefit dilemmas faced by smaller companies keen to enter the race. In addition, affordable packaged applications for customer profiling and event monitoring will decrease the advantage enjoyed up to now by larger corporations. But the inevitability of customer information fuelling the consumer markets of the future does not mean that every major consumer brand will survive into that future.

Scientific management is a term that was coined by Frederick Taylor in the early part of the 20th century and the techniques were widely applied to the administrative and production functions. Now marketing is finally about to become scientific in a very real way. Information allows us to invite and test marketing hypotheses and assumptions in ways that were not possible before. In a world where data was always incomplete the success and failures of management were subjected to the usual post hoc rationalizations. 'How were we to know?' was the plaintive cry of the US auto manufacturers, Enron investors, European telecommunications analysts and Japanese bankers at different times in the past decade. In a world where information is no longer scarce the errors of man will lie not in ignorance of the facts but in flawed assumptions concerning the facts.

There is no imminent danger of man being replaced by the cybernetic machine. And no amount of technology will replace the largely informal and complex social fabric of routine personal interaction. Man is still in charge. Man has intelligence and free will. Man has superior tools to assist decision making. Man still has the opportunity to make mistakes. But it will be a different kind of mistake. In the aftermath of disaster it is common for decision makers to characterize themselves as lost in a fog of ignorance rather than the painful truth that they were on a clearly marked landscape about which they made flawed and faulty assumptions. Information provides all the landscape markers but human ingenuity must be applied to interpreting and exploiting it.

The goal of enterprises engaged in the struggle for survival is to predict accurately and quickly the threats and opportunities that occur in their marketplace. The inherent risk associated with forecasting the future lies in the fact that there is only one accurate scenario and numerous faulty ones. Success depends on accumulating more comprehensive and integrated information in order to reduce, and ultimately eliminate, the faulty scenarios. Where the subject of the information is customers it ought to be obvious that the least faulty information will be achieved through a process of collaboration with the subject of the information. It ought also to be obvious that a systematic environment of information acquisition and analysis will precipitate a step change in the marketing function that will tip it into the domain of scientific endeavour and away from instinctive and opportunistic activities. Suppliers have been used to creating products and services and marketing them to a passive audience. In the Customer Age suppliers will increasingly respond to customer pull. Suppliers will be valued for their capabilities and responsiveness, not their products since products will increasingly be commoditized and marketing will increasingly be customized. The conventional product-centred value proposition is disappearing fast.

A survey of the amount of opposition to the notion of the customer as the owner of the relationship with the business, as opposed to the business owning the relationship with the customer, highlights many separate drivers.[10] These obstacles include organizational resistance, technology infatuation, a lack of strategic clarity, as well as, improbably but revealingly, an innate fear of the customer. Many of the dilemmas elaborated on in this book will, hopefully, assist the reader in understanding why so many customer relationship and business intelligence initiatives during the past decade have failed to meet the expectations of both the sponsoring organizations and their customers. Existing strategies for exploiting customer information are replete with fragmentation and aberration and most companies are guilty, to some extent, of sponsoring initiatives that are either blatantly contradictory (e.g. attempting to encapsulate personalization within a mass marketing framework), or cynical (e.g. buying customer loyalty or customer information with 'rewards'), or dishonest (e.g. using customer information to exploit the customer), or naïve (e.g. placing the fate of the company in technology alone). The fact that these expensive approaches are not working is apparent to virtually everyone, but criticisms of the contradictory nature of the conceptual model upon which these strategies are based is frequently drowned out by renewed demands to redouble our efforts and continue the death march that is leading so many businesses towards ethical hazard and data overload.

A conceptual framework that seeks to exclusively control information that is properly the property of customers is guaranteed to be expensive, complex, tendentious and inaccurate. Surrounding the customer citadel, manning the portals and besieging the inhabitants is not a tenable strategy for establishing relationships. The customer is not the enemy. In the long run it is not control of information *per se* but the quality of that information and the capability to exploit it will distinguish the winners. The model that has been consistently presented throughout this book is a contract where the customer explicitly exchanges meaningful and accurate information for pre-scribed benefits.

If our initial attempts at engineering a genuine dialogue between customer and suppliers have floundered, then it is here that we must renew our efforts. The guiding principle of replacing monologue with dialogue remains the enduring tendency of commercial (as well as social and political) life in this new century. Though our progress will be marked by fitful advances and occasional setbacks, it is a principle that is fated to ultimately prevail. We also need to be aware of the pitfalls of technological determinism and we neglect at our peril, the possibilities for consumers to take control of technology to empower themselves and to reshape the market for goods and services.

There is a world of difference between asserting the importance of listening to customers and ceding control of the marketing initiative to customers. Business leaders who baulk at the prospect of losing the marketing initiative will point to the need to constantly stimulate customers who are unaware of new value propositions and will point to the historical passivity of customers and prospects. But the pass-ive nature of the market in times past simply reflected the scarcity of information that was available to consumers and, in the age of the Internet, this situation no longer obtains. Consumers are not intrinsically passive and we cannot assume fundamental principles from accidental circumstances. Neither can we assert that customers, given the chance, will always decline to engage with those who are the suppliers of goods and services to them. This would not be logical from a consumer perspective, nor is there any evidence to support the validity of such fears. This tremulous logic would only be valid in circumstances where the business believed that they had no rational proposition of value to offer at all and that their business would collapse if they did not take the same measures as their competitors to constantly agitate alarm and handcuff the customer. This logic is plainly noxious. The defence of 'competitive necessity' does not dodge the logic so much as it seeks to dodge responsibility for it. So long as we continue to live in democratic societies there is no doubt about who will win the customer information wars; the customer will.

The transfer of authority to the consumer is, undeniably, a momentous proposition. It is an acknowledgement that the consumer is in charge of the relationship and that no individual consumer is an exact replica of any other consumer. It is an action that sweeps away all of the insincere posturing about 'customer relationships' by making manifest the primacy of the customer. It also has the effect of inverting many of the business processes as the entire business structure is altered from one of facilitating selling to one of facilitating buying. In so doing, many of the existing assumptions about marketing are annihilated and replaced by an entirely new grammar and vocabulary.

To the very many readers who have grown cynical of new management paradigms this author has a good deal of sympathy. Like magma churning below the earth's crust these explosions burst forth from time to time causing enormous excitement and spectacle only to subside again and be forgotten until the next eruption. But there is one very good reason to believe that the concept of the peerless customer is not fated to join the weightless economy, the cashless society or the paperless office in the growing list of premature predictions. And that very good reason is because consumers who do not receive a return on the information they provide are going to turn the information tap off entirely. And that consequence is simply not tenable for any business. Ceding control of the business relationship to the customer may still strike many readers as a radical proposition. But this timidity exists only because boldness seems always to be equated with risk when, in fact, all of history proves the contrary.

Notes

Introduction

1. Libicki, M. (1996) *What is Information Warfare?* National Defence University.
2. Toffler, A. (1980) *The Third Wave*, William Morrow.
3. Davis, S.M. (1987) *Future Perfect*, Addison Wesley.
4. Peppers, D. and Rogers, M. (1993) *The One to One Future*, Currency/Doubleday.
5. Reichheld, F. (1996) *The Loyalty Effect*, Bain & Co.
6. Kelly, S.G. (1994) *Data Warehousing: The Route to Mass Customization*, John Wiley & Sons Ltd, and (1997) *Data Warehousing in Action*, John Wiley & Sons Ltd.

1 The Concept of Customer Intelligence

1. Riddlestrale, J. and Nordstrom, K. (1999) *Funky Business*, Bookhouse Publishing AB, p. 113.
2. *Ibid*. p. 228.
3. *Coming to the Table*, (1997) Aligning the Data Warehouse with Business Objectives, Operations and Technology Council of the Advisory Board Company, p. 4.
4. *Ibid*. pp. 6–13.
5. Kelly, K. (1997) 'New Rules for the New Economy', *Wired*, September, p. 156.
6. Rothschild, M. (1995) *Bionomics: The Inevitability of Capitalism*, Henry Holt & Company provides the origin of this metaphor.
7. Kasonoff, B. (2001) *Making it Personal*, John Wiley & Sons Ltd, first refers to the concept of the 'outside in' and 'inside out' organization.

8. Levitt, T. (1983) *Harvard Business Review*, November/December.
9. Brown, S. (2001) *Marketing: The Retro Revolution*, Sage.
10. Brown, S. (2001) 'Torment Your Customers (They'll love it)', *Harvard Business Review*, October, p. 84.
11. SPAM is normally capitalized and refers to uninvited and undifferentiated mass contacts. The term derives from a bland luncheon meat product of the same name.
12. The European national flag-carriers have been devastated in the past decade by low-cost carriers, particularly by Irish airline, Ryanair, which is closely modelled on Southwest in the US.
13. Hamel, G. (2000) 'Will the "Frictionless" Economy Slip You Up?' *Wall Street Journal*, 7 June.
14. Koprowski, G. J. (2001) 'Customer Relationship Management Sheds Excess Baggage', *Wall Street Journal*, 2 November.
15. Murray, M. (1998) 'Bank with a Giant or Bank with MertonCorn', *Wall Street Journal* 28 August.
16. Shaw, R. (1999) *CRM at the Crossroads*, Sybase Inc. White Paper.
17. It was E. Jerome McCarthy who in the 1950s developed the mnemonic, the 'four Ps' which has become the most enduring of the marketing mix frameworks.
18. Reichheld, F. (1994) *Marketing Management*, 2(4), p. 10.

2 Achieving an Intelligence Capability

1. John Zachman, who worked for IBM, wrote extensively and with extraordinary prescience about the impending dangers of un-architected information systems throughout the 1980s.
2. Porter, M.E. (1990) *The Competitive Advantage of Nations*, The Free Press, pp. 48–49.
3. Drucker, P.F. (1994) *Knowledge Work and Knowledge Society – The Social Transformation of this Century*, Edwin L. Godkin Lecture, 4 May.
4. *Crossing the Millennium*, Palo Alto Management Group Inc.
5. Shannon, C. (1948) 'A Mathematical Theory of Communication', *Bell System Technical Journal*, vol. 27. This article formed the basis of information theory.
6. Bernstein, P.L. (1996) *Against the Gods: The Remarkable Story of Risk*, John Wiley & Sons Ltd, is the main text from which this list is culled.

This book is highly recommended for the general reader who is investigating further into the application of intelligence to information.

7. *Ibid.*

8. Krugman, P. (1999) *The Return of Depression Economics*, Penguin, p. 98.

9. Hagstrom, R.G. (1995) *The Warren Buffett Way*, John Wiley & Sons Ltd, p. 258.

10. Coyle, D. (1997) *The Weightless World: Strategies for Managing the Digital Economy*, Capstone.

11. 2001 monograph by Richard Hackathorn, director of Business Intelligence at Enterprise Management Associates.

12. Kelly, S.G. (1994) *Data Warehousing:The Route to Mass Customization*, John Wiley & Sons Ltd, p. 55, provides this conceptual definition and it appears to have stood the test of time.

13. Readers wishing to track the price performance of query-based database engines are referred to the annual reports of the Winter Corporation, Waltham, MA.

14. Berry, M. and Linoff, G. (1997) *Data Mining Techniques for Marketing, Sales and Customer Suppport*, John Wiley & Sons Ltd, p. 5.

15. This definition was agreed at the first KDD (Knowledge Discovery in Data) conference in Montreal in 1995.

16. Adriaans, P. and Zantinge, D. (1996) *Data Mining*, Addison Wesley, p. 13.

17. The Data Warehousing Institute. 2001 study surveyed more than 1,670 business executives and IT professionals.

18. Kelly, S.G. (1994) *Data Warehousing:The Route to Mass Customization*, John Wiley & Sons Ltd.

19. Larry English.

20. A 2004 IBM study on *Doing CRM Right* is the latest piece of research to show that change management is still the number one roadblock to success.

21. For this riposte I am indebted to Bill Inmon, which he delivered when we both shared a panel at the Business Intelligence 2002 conference in Sao Paulo.

22. McKean, J. (1999) *Information Masters*, John Wiley & Sons Ltd, p. 93. Similar evidence of the failure of business intelligence projects can be found in numerous other sources including the annual estimates provided each year by the Gartner Group, the Meta Group, the Data Warehousing Institute (US), the Data Warehouse Network (Europe) and IDC.

3 The Eclipse of Mass Marketing

1. Davis, S.M. (1987) *Future Perfect*, Addison Wesley, p. 28.
2. Swift, R. (2001) *Business – Creating Increased Profitability Through CRM*, Ascet, vol. 2, 15 August.
3. Fukuyama, F. (1992) *The End of History and the Last Man*, Avon Books Inc., pp. 240–244.
4. Source: R.L. Polk (1997), Manufacturers' Loyalty Survey.
5. *Time* (2000), 'The Virtual Grocer', 30 October, p. 88.
6. This figure is an average of the composite estimates for the traditional and e-CRM markets provided by Gartner Group, AMR research and e-marketer in the period 2000/2001.
7. This figure is based on an estimate of $19.9bn for 2000 provided by the Gartner Group.
8. Source: Dataquest 2001.
9. Porter, M. (1980) *Competitive Strategies*, The Free Press, pp. 19–30.
10. Leaders in this field include Tesco in Europe and Sears in the US.
11. This specific risk was identified as early as 1986 in *Managing in the Service Economy*, by James L. Heskett, Harvard Business School Press.
12. Levitt, T. (1975) 'Retrospective commentary on *Marketing Myopia*', *Harvard Business Review*, September/October.
13. Reichheld, F. (1996) *The Loyalty Effect*, Harvard Business School Press, p. 39.
14. I am indebted to Bent Svanholmer for sharing his expertise in measuring lifetime value as published in *Kundeloyaliet*, 1996, Borsen.

4 Achieving Segmentation and Differentiation

1. Casserley, D. (1991) *Facing Up to the Risks*, John Wiley & Sons Ltd, p. 125.
2. *Online Influencers Rely on Company Websites*, CyberAtlas, 26 December 2001.
3. The first investigations in this field of research were produced by the Chicago urban sociologists, Park and Burgess, in the 1920s.

4. Brown, P.J.B. (2003) *Reflections on a further decade of developments in geo-demographics*, presented to the 50th North American Meeting of the Regional Science Association International, Philadelphia, November 2003.
5. This term 'contented class' was coined by John Kenneth Galbraith in *The Culture of Contentment* (1992), Vintage/Ebury. The 'two thirds society' was a term coined in 1993 by Peter Glotz, a German politician of the Social Democratic Party.
6. Levinson, M. (2000) 'Slices of Lives', *CIO Magazine*, 15 August.
7. Quoted in *Forbes Magazine* 23 February 1998, p. 90.

5 The Collapse of Time

1. This term is attributed to investment firm Integral Capital Partners where the term was first encountered.
2. Davis, S. and Mcycr, C. (1998) *Blur*, Warncr Books.
3. This pertinent issue was posed and explored by Dr. S.K. Chakraborty of the Management Centre for Human Value Systems, Calcutta, India speaking at the Scandinavian Interactive Media Event (SIMA) in June 2000.
4. Henry, D. and Vickers, M. (2003) 'Whipsawed by Wall Street', *Business Week* cover story, 10 March, p. 45.

6 Customer Privacy and Confidentiality

1. From *Business Week*, 'Why Service Stinks', 23 October 2001.
2. Friedman, T.L. (2000) *The Lexus and the Olive Tree*, Anchor Books, p. 426.
3. Foroohar, R. (2004) 'The Future of Shopping', *Newsweek*, June 7–14, p. 77. Quotation attributed to Katherine Albrecht, founder of the US-based privacy group CASPIAN.
4. Top 10 strategic IT initiatives in e-CRM for the New Millennium, 2000 Meridian Research.

5. These definitions are based on those that appear in the final report of the advisory committee of the US Fair Trade Commission on Online Security and Access released on 15 May 2000.

6. Mason, R. (1986) 'Four Ethical Issues of the Information Age', *MIS Quarterly* 10(1), pp. 5–12. This essay has been very influential in the subsequent literature.

7. Source: Etrade.

8. US Supreme Court Appeal 397 US 728 Rowan, DBA American Book Service *et al.* v. United States Post Office Department *et al.* Appeal From the United States District Court for the Central District of California No. 399. Argued 22 Jan. 1970. Decided 4 May 1970.

9. Peter Swire, an Ohio State University professor of law speaking on 16 October 1998 at a Brookings Institute luncheon.

10. Fukuyama, F. (1992) *The End of History and the Last Man*, Avon Books Inc., pp.240–244.

11. George Howarth, the British Home Office minister reported in the *Daily Telegraph*, 4 August 1998.

12. 108th Congress (2003–2004) CAN-SPAM Act of 2003 (S. 877).

13. EU Directive No. 2002/58/EC European Communities (Electronic Communications Networks and services) (Data Protection and Privacy) Regulations 2003-12-22.

14. Testimony given before the Senate Committee on Commerce, Science and Transportation on 25 May 2000. This testimony is the subject of review in Chapter 3 of Bruce Kasanoff (2001), *Making it Personal*, John Wiley & Sons Ltd.

15. Godin, S. (1999) *Permission Marketing*, Simon & Schuster.

16. Bill Gates quoted in 'Market of One' by John Foley, *Information Week*, 17 February 1997, p. 36.

17. This sample is taken from a note filed with the SEC by strategy.com in 1999.

18. This summary of viewpoints is culled from the Final Report of the FTC Advisory Committee on Online Access and Security 15 May 2000.

19. Fukuyama, F. (1996) *Trust: Social Virtues and the Creation of Prosperity*, Penguin/Putnam.

7 Closing the Loop

1. Kelly, S. (2002) *Dialogue & Segmentation*, Comhrá White Paper.
2. Reichheld, F. F. (2003) 'The One Number You Need', *Harvard Business Review*, December, p. 47.

8 The New Practice of Marketing

1. Bernstein, P. L. (1996) *Against the Gods: The Remarkable Story of Risk*, John Wiley & Sons Ltd, p. 329.
2. This description of the chess endgame is attributed to Sawielly Grigoriewitsch Tartakower (1887–1956), chess grandmaster.
3. Burlton, R. (2001) *Business Process Management*, Sams Publishing.
4. Wayland, R.E. and Cole, P.M. (1997) *Customer Connections*, Harvard Business School.
5. Eco, U. (1999) *Serendipities*, Orion Books, p. 97.
6. One of the first observations on this topic was that of Sun Microsystems' co-founder and chief scientist Bill Joy in an article in *Wired* that appeared in April 2000.
7. *Ibid.*
8. This point has been elaborated on by Tom Peters in a number of publications.
9. McKean, J. (1999) *Information Masters*, John Wiley & Sons Ltd, p. XX.
10. From *New Wave of Intelligent Commerce* survey conducted by Comhrá.com in 2003.

Index